Luis Wester

Blockchain Maximalist

English Version

OnePeople.io Publishing

"It's going to be bigger than you thought, it's going to happen quicker than you imagined, and it's going to be more rewarding than you ever dreamed of."

Unknown

Visit the books website:
BlockchainMaximalist.com

Visit the OnePeople.io website:
OnePeople.io

1.2 Paperback Edition 2019
English Version by Luis Wester
Original Version by Luis Wester
Font: Times New Roman and Trajan Pro
eBook Version available here:
https://www.amazon.com/dp/B07NVTBYGG
Printed by Amazon
ISBN 978-1-797-458991

Contents

Blockchain Maximalist

[blok-cheyn **mak**-s*uh*-m*uh*-list]

noun

An individual that firmly believes in the revolutionary potential and world-changing impact of Blockchain and that the surrounding technologies hold the key to a new, decentralized era of a global and interconnected civilization.

Introduction

We have entered a radical evolution of how we interact and trade in an ever-more interconnected world. The transformation to public self-governance has already begun and will result in a restructure and redistribution of power and control in society. It is greeted with fear from many of the traditional institutions, which try their absolute most to cling onto their established power through regulations and public opinion campaigns. All these efforts, all across the earth will fail. One by one, organizations must adapt or be replaced. The shift into the new decentralized era is underway.

As a child, I often pondered my place in the universe and often wished to have been born at a different period in time. I wanted to live during a time of discovery and adventure, in the distant past I could've explored new continents and countries, seen places never before seen by another human, scaled mountains that have never before been scaled, sailed oceans to new civilizations, and watched discoveries like electricity completely change the face of the earth. A hundred years into the future I could be a part of the planetary exploration of our solar system and beyond and see technologies unfold that would be considered black magic today.

I've immersed myself fully in the concepts surrounding some of the major technological advances of the past two decades and the deeper I traveled down this rabbit hole; the clearer was the image that emerged. An image of a global, borderless, self-governing civilization, built on a new form of information networks.

A genuinely universal economic system that is for the first time, in harmony with its underlying technology.

I have not wished of a different place in time for quite a while now and throughout these next pages; I hope to bring forth the same flame inside of you, that has been driving me about the time that we live in.

Societies have been kicking the can in front of themselves for far too long now. There are significant issues that we have delayed, postponed, or straight up ignored in greed for short-term gain. Centralized organizations and institutions control the majority of our data and repeatedly abuse it. Government-issued currencies have long lost any connection to actual value and are inflated continuously by the minting of new bills. The annual inflation rate of the Dollar was 2.44% in 2018 according to the Bureau of Labor Statistics, Former Federal Reserve Board Chairman Alan Greenspan recently stated in an interview that, *"when in-*

flation goes up to 4% to 5%, it is politically disastrous. That's when it becomes an issue. But when it starts rising, it's already too late in the game to stabilize it." The Euro was inflated by 1.67% in 2018 according to the statistics published by Eurostat and the Venezuelan Bolívar inflated by 2,616% in 2017 and, according to Professor Hanke, the inflation rate of the VES rose to over 1,370,000% in 2018. Venezuela, Turkey, Iran, Yemen, Somalia, Mozambique, and Zimbabwe are only the first of a long list of countries in the world currently undergoing economic disasters and with a dying fiat currency will need to look elsewhere for a trusted or trustless model.

The United States is run by a president that lost the popular vote, and the Syrian refugee crisis has unveiled countless administrative flaws in the European governments and state-based identification. International tensions are increasing through unnecessary trade war hostility, originating from the US. Black Rock chairman and CEO Larry Fink expressed his concerns about the US-China trade war, "*Generally when you fight with your banker, it's not a good outcome.*"

The recent attempted tax increases on fuel by president Macron enraged hundreds of thousands of protestors in France. The yellow vest uprising turned violent in Paris, resulting in four deaths and hundreds injured. The advent of Trump and Brexit signifies a step backward in history.

We are for the first time in recent history shifting away from a global perspective in favor of a national one. Nationalism, however, does not provide a solution for global problems such as the emergence of a 'useless' class due to artificial intelligence, global warming, genetic engineering, and other high-risk, high-reward, scientific endeavors. Only a global authority can act upon these.

We cannot let the emotional, irrational individuals make this decision for us. The current economic and political models are unfit to deal with the technological disruptions of the 21st century and are thus unable to serve as a foundation for a global, borderless, and free community. Too much in this world has already been lost to the unfathomable ego and hubris of little men. We need to change the systems.

Centralized institutions, organizations, and governments have served their purpose over the last centuries, but it is time to move on and advance into a new form of global services and information economy. To overcome the challenges and misrepresentation that have plagued us in the past, we will replace the economic model of the industrial age. We, the people give these institutions power over our lives, because until now, we had no other option. No way to ensure our security without giving up our privacy and freedom. We do now.

The emerging global economy will consist of coordinated protocols that provide a secure and distributed infrastructure. The evolution builds upon major, previously divergent trends that began in the late 20th. century which Blockchain has merged in compelling new ways.

The fastest way to get more people onboard the Blockchain bandwagon is to inform and educate them in the most simplistic way possible. This way barriers are broken, bridges built, and the myth of Blockchain unraveled on a global scale.

It is a valid argument that one of the biggest threats to the pace of growth of Blockchain is the seemingly complex nature of the technology. The natural assumption by anyone that is not IT-inclined is to dismiss Blockchain as an overtly advanced and 'not-in-my-league' type of technology when in fact there's a whole lot to be gained from its use, by everyone, and the underlying concepts are more comfortably grasped than one might assume.

Blockchain gives us back the control over our data, of which governments and enterprises like Facebook and Google have made nearly unrestricted, leisurely use so far. Our privacy and anonymity, violated on a regular basis. Technology itself will be the driving force that returns the power back to the people.

The most challenging problem that individuals will face in the coming years is a combination of how they think about their place in society, how these emerging technologies function, and how they will beneficially impact their own lives.

Blockchain's full application as a decentralized database is monumental and has already been received with varying degrees of acceptance and attitude. Blockchains' decentralizing nature literally puts the tools to succeed in an interconnected world without banks or central governments into our pockets.

Our civilization as a whole is at the brink of societal evolution and the speed of the revolution only depends on one single factor, adoption. Adoption of the new ways of life.

This book is intended to serve as a scientifically accurate accession to the existing pool of knowledge and to give you the ability to view our future in a bright and comfortable light. Addressing those who are in need of further convincing in what I hope is a fascinating journey of discoveries and aspiring to revise our cultural appreciation of Blockchain, which has deteriorated in the recent past.

Personally, I am in love with these revolutionary technologies and discovering their new facets and deeper layers. I am mesmerized by the idea of the unification of humanity through technology.

Before we continue, I would like to make a final comment on the structure of this book. To explore potential applications that illustrate the monumental impact of Blockchain, we need to establish a solid foundation by firmly grasping some of the underlying concepts. The book is structured to streamline this process. The chapters are written in a logical sequence transversing a narrative arc in three main parts.

Part one demystifies the underlying technologies and some of the different protocols surrounding Blockchain and accumulates to the first educational and informative section in this book. It will serve as an introduction to, and refresher of, some of the fundamental concepts behind the mentioned technologies while also detailing some of their functions and mechanics. We will disentangle Blockchain, Smart Contracts, and Consensus Mechanisms in particular while briefly touching upon other essential topics. In part one, we build a foundational layer on which the succeeding parts are built.

Part two elaborates on the challenges that Blockchain had to face thus far and what we can expect in the future. We will discuss several interesting and infamous breakthroughs, discoveries, and advancements. We will examine concepts like Double-Spending and the Byzantine Generals' Problem in detail. This part makes clear how far the technology has come, where we currently stand in society, and what challenges we will face going forward. It includes a detailed and structured timeline of significant milestones that Blockchain has achieved, like the conceptualization of a timestamped series of blocks in 1991 by Stuart Haber and W. Scott Stornetta and May 22, 2010, Pizza Day, the day of the first real-world transaction on a Blockchain.

Part three unpacks the obvious reasons why this emerging technology will fundamentally restructure our society. It is a safe passage from the challenges and advantages of Blockchain in part one and two to the applications and explores several concepts and ideas that will have a monumental effect on our day-to-day lives. We will take an intricate look at how these new technologies accommodate the individual in an ever-more connected society. We will explore some philosophical implications of Blockchain-enabled direct democratic governance and establish the revolutionary potential and world-changing effect of the surrounding technologies as the key to a new, decentralized era of a global and interconnected civilization.

Concluding the book with a polarizing critique of the current economic models but with genuine, optimistic anticipation. In this final closure, I will leave the objectivity of the previous parts behind and indulge in some opinionated, first-person criticism addressed to some of the major institutions governing our lives.

Part one and two of the book, are intended, not only to provide a foundation, but also insights into what technological concepts are taken into consideration to arrive at the conclusions of part three. I hope to clearly demonstrate which concepts distort my own vision, writing, and way in which I see the world.

I should point out that you need not listen to these parts in this progressive, three-part narrative and each part can essentially be listened to individually and out of order without losing much of its significance.

We encounter the word Blockchain, upper case, several times in these pages, which is not only referring to a time-stamped series of blocks, usually written in the lower case, but includes all of the surrounding infrastructure of Smart Contracts and Consensus Mechanisms.

I will strive to stay away from naming specific coins and companies as I do not intend to shill any cryptoasset. If I do refer to particular projects I do so out of necessity and in an objective manner, it does not imply endorsement of any kind.

Scattered throughout this book are a useful amount of supplementary material and references to various media articles, videos, and other information, which can be found in a convenient format at the book's website. Blockchain-Maximalist.com

Throughout our journey, you will notice my proclivity to include various relevant and significant quotes in my writing, whenever I get the chance. To which I will respond by borrowing words from Michel de Montaigne, *"I quote others in order to better express myself."*

A personal note about my goal with this book.

Essentially, I want you to feel and experience three primary emotions throughout our journey in these pages. Firstly, I want you to feel educated. That you are both informed and knowledgeable about Blockchain, the technology, and the possibilities. Secondly, I aim to empower you, by providing practical and applicable information in a clear and precise manner. That you no longer fear or question the changes that are occurring on a global scale. Lastly, my main intention with these words is to inspire you, to stimulate your mind with the vision of the impact of these technologies. To inspire you in such a visceral way that we ignite the same flame inside of you that has kept me up at night in excitement, optimism, and eagerness about the changes we will face in the near future.

That you are aware and educated, empowered and inspired so profoundly that you firmly believe in the revolutionary impact of Blockchain and that you, yourself, take action and advance the adoption of it.

This book is the result of years of dedication and curiosity and strives to elaborate the underlying concepts amply enough for you to embark on this journey yourself while saving months of your own research.

Understand the underlying concepts, and you will understand the technology.

If you are someone who would like to grasp some of the deeper layers of one of the most revolutionary technologies of our time, then this book is for you.

"Any sufficiently advanced technology is indistinguishable from magic."

Arthur C. Clarke

Part 1

One chain to rule them all

The radical potential of Blockchain technology has long spread outside the world of crypto into the hands of the general public. We've all heard through one way or another that it is most likely the most revolutionary technology that is presently available in any known market and that includes the real-world as well as the digital space. As you might be aware by now, Blockchain technology is principally behind the emergence of Bitcoin and many other cryptocurrencies and assets that are too numerous to mention.

Blockchain is not a company, an organization, or an app; it is a completely new way of documenting data on the internet. The information documented on these chains can take any form, such as a transaction, an agreement between two parties, ownership, or even someone's identity and thus enables the emergence of a new type of decentralized application that ranges from voting systems to exchanges, social networks to prediction markets, and much more. In its range of application, it parallels the internet.

The fascination and the interest in the technology have seen an unprecedented rise in the number of searches for Blockchain made on search engines in recent times. As a matter of fact, it is on record that Blockchain related searches on the Google engine have spiraled by as much as 1900% since 2013, peaking in December 2017 and January 2018 and recently again in November of 2018.

The Blockchain revolution looks set to flip the status quo of centralized systems in most industries for a more decentralized, transparent, open, fair, secure, efficient, and democratic infrastructure. While most people view Blockchain from a transactional perspective and rightly so, there are still many salient aspects of a true Blockchain structure that people have not paid particular attention to.

These facets, however, are responsible for the nature of the technology as we know it and the reason why its set to revolutionize the way people transact with others in the near and distant future. They are what really should endear the mainstream to its use.

Blockchain is changing our society on a fundamental level. It is transforming what we can do online, how we do it, and who can participate. We will examine the three pillars of the Blockchain infrastructure next; blockchain (lower case), smart contracts, and consensus mechanisms. A cryptographically secured peer-to-peer network is what these pillars are built upon.

With the development of Blockchain technology, we have created a tool to completely alter hierarchal infrastructures and by so doing make them a whole lot more effective, efficient, dependable, and resilient.

The following section is arguably the most densely packed and information heavy part of this book, and I do understand the inexistent allure of such a loaded part at the beginning. Establishing a common foundation of knowledge, however, is absolutely essential to the context of the later parts.

Blockchains

A distributed ledger is a database that is held and frequently updated independently by every participating computer or device operating in the network. These separately owned computers can be referred to as nodes, and the distribution of these nodes can be described as nothing short of exquisite: no central authority is responsible for communicating records to the different nodes, but rather records are independently generated and kept by each node. Distributed ledgers have been created due to innovations in cryptography as well as access to vast computing power and the availability of fascinating, new algorithms.

The genuinely independent nodes help to record, share, and synchronize every transaction in a particular electronic ledger which is different from a traditional ledger in which a central authority is responsible for the security and storage.

Blockchain is a type of Distributed Ledger Technology. The terminology has become interchangeable, and Blockchain has become a ubiquitous reference to the technology as a whole. In the Blockchain community, it is accepted, although not universally, that DLTs are included in the encompassing terminology of Blockchain and not the other way around. The distinct differences between other types of ledgers are interesting to explore, however, negligible for our sake.

Blockchain technology is a decentralized database that stores a registry of transactions and assets across a peer-to-peer network. As Bettina Warburg states in her recent TED talk, *"It is basically a public registry of who owns what and who transacts what."* These transactions are secured through cryptography and stored in an expanding series of blocks of data that are linked together in an 'append only' mode. This creates an immutable and unforgeable record of all transactions on the network that is replicated and secured on every computer that uses it.

There has always been a dire need to be able to certify when a document was created and last modified, for intellectual property, for example, it is vital to be able to confirm the validity of any particular information. The need for a method of certification and validation grew exponentially with the advent of the internet and digital documents. All of a sudden, nearly all new media was easily modifiable and duplicable. Not knowing when any particular file was created and last modified made the internet unfit for many intellectual and legal contracts and documents. This is why until now, the majority of transactions are still sealed through a signature on a hard copy: property purchases, legal agreements, rental and lease contracts, business filings. The issue is the time-stamping of the data itself and not the medium. Hard papers usually include a date of creation and a date of signing. Digital contracts can be altered retrospectively.

To truly grasp and understand the potential impact of the technology we need to understand its fundamental components which are too many of us, still a bit mysterious.

One component of the Blockchain foundation is the **Hash** function. A hash function maps data of arbitrary size to a fixed size through a mathematical algorithm. According to Paul Snow, CEO of Factom, "*Very simply, a hash acts like a unique fingerprint for anything digital. Much like your* *own fingerprint, a hash is a unique identification for any digital thing. There is a unique hash for a picture, an MP3 file or really anything else you can think of that you might have on a computer.*"

This fingerprint is unique and entirely dependent on the source data. Any modification of any part of the input will result in an entirely different hash. Anyone input only has one single output. It will not match anything else. Hashing is not 'encrypting' which means it cannot be decrypted back to the original text. It is a 'one-way' cryptographic function.

The image titled 'Hash Functions' on the book's website looks as follows. On the left, there is a text block representing a transaction, labeled input. It contains a transaction amount and a recipient. The recipient is an arbitrary 34 letter long alphanumerical string, while the transaction amount is a four-digit numeric, 2.356. There is an arrow in the center, pointing to the text block on the right, labeled output. A 64 letter long alphanumerical string.

1db1f623ca2caad82fcf182813c129c65f308c7166b9d6594b066228b324ec3f

There are many online converters available, and I recommend you try out at least one of them. www.tools4noobs.com/online_tools/hash/ is one, but a google search will yield plenty of viable options. SHA 256 is one of the most commonly used hash functions in Blockchain cryptography, but all chains use some form of hashing. SHA-256 generates an almost-unique 256-bit (32-byte) signature for a text. This Secure Hash Algorithm was designed by the NSA and has not yet been compromised in any way.

In 1991, Stuart Haber and W. Scott Stornetta were intent on developing a mechanism whereby the timestamps of documents are permanent and cannot in any way be altered. Haber and Stornetta were the first to propose a computationally practical procedure for digital time-stamping, so that it is infeasible for a user either to back-date or to forward-date his document, even with the collusion of a time-stamping service.

The two provided research work for a chain of records (blocks) that are secured cryptographically. The procedure removes the need for any third-party validation or record-keeping service while maintaining complete privacy of the documents themselves.

Now with this early blockchain template on ground; Dave Bayer, Haber, and Stornetta deployed **Merkle Hash Trees** to the overall design in order to vastly improve its level of efficiency and effectiveness by permitting a large number of transactions or documents to be collated in a single block in the chain.

The Merkle Tree allows you to efficiently verify transactions without having to scan the body of every block, while still providing a way to validate the entire blockchain on every transaction.

To grasp this concept more easily, let's unpack it into its different components. Consider a block with eight transactions. The transactions are the lowest level of the tree. Each of the transactions is hashed through a mathematical hash function. The transaction hashes are the leaves of the tree. Two or more of these leaves are each connected to a branch on the next level. These branches are the hashes of their leaves, and the branches on the next level of the tree are the hashes of their respective children and so on until the top of the tree is reached which contains the top hash, often referred to as the root or master hash.

The root hash of a Merkle Tree is the hash of all hashes in the block. Merkle Hash Trees allow efficient and secure verification that a transaction has been accepted by the network by verifying just the small block header without verifying all of the contents of the data structure.

A block contains a unique header used to identify it on a blockchain. It is the hash of a combination of data including the Merkle root hash, the hash of the previous block header, a timestamp, and further chain specific data. This is the mechanism that links blocks together in a chain.

For example, the Bitcoin block header contains the Bitcoin version number used to keep track of changes in the protocol, a timestamp which is the number of seconds passed since January 1970 (minus leap seconds), a difficulty target and nonce which are used in Bitcoin's Proof-of-Work algorithm, more on this later, in addition to the hash of the previous block and the Merkle root hash.

The Bitcoin header is an 80-byte long string. It comprises of the 4-byte long Bitcoin version number, 32-byte previous block hash, 32-byte long Merkle root, 4-byte long timestamp of the block, 4-byte long difficulty target for the block, and 4-byte long nonce used by miners.

Blockchains are therefore open and distributed ledgers that are capable of effectively recording the transactions that occur between two parties in a verifiable, efficient, and somewhat permanent manner.

When the blockchain is utilized as a distributed ledger it is generally under the management of a peer-to-peer network that confirms, validates, and authenticates new blocks while remaining in compliance with an inter-node communication protocol.

Within peer-to-peer infrastructure, the user generally both utilizes as well as provides the foundation of the network. Providing the resources, however, is usually voluntary as users refuse to provide resources if the incentive is not convincing enough.

The peers in such a network, are the nodes. In reality, though, these networks draw no distinction between autonomous computers and humans. The use of the euphemism, however, is understandable, as 'node-to-node' network sounds far less appealing.

A compelling advantage of peer-to-peer infrastructure over traditional client-server models is the improved speed of decentralized system with the increase in users. Additionally, the manner in which the connection is established minimizes resource use, making it possible for microcomputers to occupy spaces in these networks. Traditional systems tend to slow down with an increase in traffic. The capacity-related issue with Macy's website and credit card gateways during Black Friday of 2017 spring to mind and these issues are likely more common than you think. The efficiency of a peer-to-peer network grows with its expansion. The more nodes in a network the faster and more secure it will be.

No central authority can censor these networks and push their own agenda. Instead, the user is in control and, given that the chain is appropriately secured, becomes the true owner of their personal data.

It is a tool we can use to free ourselves of social networks in which the company owns all of our data. (cough) Facebook. And of banks and payment gateways that control access to our funds and can restrict it as they seem fit.

Depending on the network, these nodes can take on distinct and different roles. They may not all be equal. The Bitcoin Blockchain comprises of regular, 'lightweight' nodes, which are users, and 'full' nodes, which as miner nodes require the entire blockchain to be downloaded onto a computer to store, secure, and update the information.

These full nodes are the reason why no central point of storage is required, reducing the risk of data being stolen or destroyed. All the information is stored and secured on countless devices around the world. Attacking or destroying a single point of storage results in no loss of data. Additionally, the lack of central servers and authorities means that there is no central point of failure that can lose power or be hacked to change the data inside of any block.

To destroy the information stored on a Blockchain, you would need to destroy every full node in the network. A single full node is enough to rebuild it with all data intact.

Blockchains that are readable and accessible to the general public are mainly utilized by open networks and digital assets or cryptocurrencies such as Bitcoin and Ethereum, whereas most enterprises and businesses prefer the use of private blockchains which have a limited range of accessibility.

The Blockchain infrastructure is designed to resist any alteration to the transaction data once the data is recorded, as any change would lead to modifications to future blocks added to the chain. For any alteration to the transaction data in a block to take effect, there must be a consensus in the network quorum.

But even though the blocks of the blockchain can be modified by consensus, they are generally designed to be a secure, distributed, computing mechanism with a high Byzantine Fault Tolerance, about which you will learn more in Part Two.

The decentralized nature of Blockchain and the lack of a single authority makes the system fairer and significantly more secure. If Blockchain structures were centralized, the technology would likely not be necessary. This is how critical the decentralization is. It is the foundation on which Blockchain technology is built and is responsible for some of its significant benefits, which include: resistance to censorship, immutability, and trustlessness.

The open and transparent nature of these networks makes it very apparent to the public if and what data is accessible and if there is any censorship occurring. The fact that these networks are not centrally controlled or managed means that governments can't exercise any judicial or legislative power over them. The Blockchain structure comprises of systems that are independent of centralized third-party participation in the safekeeping and storage of both data and assets.

The data is made even more secure through cryptography, utilized as a means of protecting the identities of users and ensuring that transactions are processed securely and stored permanently. Users in the network can have complete confidence that their data and transactions are recorded in an accurate and untampered manner. We need strong cryptography so we can trust that our communications can only be seen by the people we want. There are many well-tested options for this, including newer approaches built to resist attacks even from quantum computers.

Asymmetric or public-key cryptography is an essential component of many cryptoassets like Bitcoin and Ethereum. These advanced cryptographic techniques ensure that the source of a transaction is legitimate and the information protected from hackers.

The Public Key Cryptographic System relies on a pair of keys, a private key, which is ideally kept secret, and a public key, which is broadcasted out to the network.

In the Bitcoin protocol, public-key cryptography is utilized in several places to ensure the integrity of transactions.

Bitcoin relies on the Elliptic Curve Digital Signature Algorithm (ECDSA) to create the set of private and public keys. The public key is hashed to generate the public address which is used to send and receive funds. The private key is used to sign a transaction to ensure it's origin is legitimate.

By combining the users' private key with the desired data that they wish to sign through a mathematical algorithm a digital signature is created. The hash of the actual information itself is part of the signature, ensuring the network will not validate it if the data has been modified. Altering even the slightest aspect of it reshapes the whole signature, making it false and obsolete. Digital signatures are what give the data recorded on a Blockchain its immutability.

This mechanism is there to verify that the author of the transaction is, in fact, the individual holding the private key. In this way, a digital signature is quite similar to an actual signature on a document.

Digital signatures are the backbone of the majority of Blockchain projects and depend on two functions.

The signing and the verifying of transactions. To sign, we combine the transaction or message with our private key producing our unique digital signature.

Sign(Hash of Transaction Data, Private Key) -> Digital Signature

Once a transaction is signed by the author, it is sent to the memory pool where it awaits processing. Dedicated nodes use the senders public key to ensure that the digital signature is authentic without access to the contents of the message or the private key.

Verify(Public Key, Signature) -> True/False

This function results in a binary output of True or False. If the ownership is confirmed, the transaction is included in the next block and once processed, the information is sent from one address to the other.

This confirmation function is referred to as a 'Consensus Mechanism' which ultimately dismisses the need for users to 'trust' third-parties in the transaction of their funds and data.

The original consensus mechanism available in a truly decentralized Blockchain structure is 'Proof-of-Work' or PoW. The PoW algorithm ratifies transactions and generates new blocks to be included in the chain. PoW brings limitless decentralized nodes together in perfect harmony and in a synchronized manner. It is, however, reliant on substantial computing power to resolve very complicated mathematical puzzles. More on these mechanisms later.

We are now aware of the components that comprise a block in a blockchain. We understand that the information and transactions are hashed and then stored in an efficient Merkle Tree structure and how the different blocks are chained together by including the hash of the previous block header in the current one. We also examined certain, common cryptographic functions that are responsible for the private and anonymous nature of the technology. This knowledge will help us on our journey later on.

The first pillar, blockchain, is responsible for the security and storage of data. We will inspect how this data and information is exchanged and transacted next.

Smart Contracts

The second pillar of Blockchain which drastically enhances its ability to fundamentally disrupt a variety of industries, is smart contracts. Smart contracts are contracts written in code and embedded onto a particular blockchain; they are occasionally referred to as self-executing contracts, blockchain contracts, or digital contracts. The code within these contracts contains all the rules, conditions, expiry dates and all other relevant information needed for its fulfillment, which executes automatically once the terms are met.

As opposed to traditional contracts, a smart contract includes conditions pre-written in a precise mathematical language which is very different to ones based on human language, which can be very subjective and open to judicial interpretation. Instead, a smart contract behaves in predefined ways and is automated in the pattern of 'if this happens, then do that,' which is a more objective, data-driven way to ensure contract conditions are met.

What makes smart contracts so crucial to expanding Blockchain use cases is the fact that the conditions for completion and requirements of all parties are entirely quantifiable. This means that a specific numerical action needs to take place in order for the smart contract to be executed, revoked, or terminated.

Smart contracts are algorithms which are designed to secure, execute, and implement the resolution of a contract existing between individuals and organizations in an automated manner. They are digital agreements between parties that are trackable and irreversible and allow the conduction and performance of credible transactions without any third-party.

It was Nick Szabo, a legal scholar and cryptographer, that first proposed and coined the term Smart Contracts, back in 1994. Szabo drew a comparison to a digital vending machine: you select an item, input the required amount of cash, and receive the desired goods when the payment is registered. In his paper, he proposed the execution of a contract for synthetic assets, such as derivatives and bonds. *"These new securities are formed by combining securities (such as bonds) and derivatives (options and futures) in a wide variety of ways. Very complex term structures for payments can now be built into standardized contracts and traded with low transaction costs[...]."*

With smart contracts items of value, including shares, property, and money can easily be exchanged. Furthermore, the exchange is done without the need for intermediaries in a trustless, open, fair, transparent, and also dispute-free manner. Szabo himself describes them as, *"... a computerized transaction protocol that executes the terms of a contract. The general objectives of smart contract design are to satisfy common contractual conditions, minimize exceptions both malicious and accidental, and minimize the need for trusted intermediaries."*

While the distributed Blockchain ledger dispenses third-parties in the storing and securing of data and assets, smart contracts do so in the transaction of these items. Without the need for third-party participation, middlemen such as lawyers and brokers, are entirely redundant. You also don't have to worry about the common errors experienced with more manual forms of contracts which involve the filling and filing of various forms and hence increasing the propensity for mistakes. The final decision on any smart contract transaction rests with the participants of the contract. Third-parties cannot alter or manipulate the contract as it is automatically generated within the Blockchain network. The software codes utilized by smart contracts ensure that tasks are fully automated and this saves a considerable amount of business transaction processing time.

All documents are encrypted on the chain which renders the problem of misplacement a non-issue as the data of individuals is duplicated numerously and stored securely. The encryption ensures that all data is kept safe and secure from the threat of hackers and other cybercriminals.

Let's consider the fact that ownership merely is recognition by a government or agency that you own something and they will defend your claims on that ownership. Property rights, both real and intellectual, are a prime example. We will no longer require governments and other central authorities to oversee our individual property rights. We can now replace them with systems that require no trust at all. The ownership is verified automatically, and we can transact them freely, globally, and anonymously.

Don and Alex Tapscott, two of the most vocal and simultaneously most profound voices in the space, elaborate a prime example in their 2016 publication, Blockchain Revolution, detailing that smart contracts, "... *provide a means of assigning usage rights to another party. As a composer might assign a completed song to a music publisher. The code of the contract could include the term or the duration of the assignment, the magnitude of royalties that would flow from the publishers to the composer's Bitcoin account during the term and some triggers for terminating the contract.*

For example, if the composer's account receives less than a quarter of a Bitcoin in a consecutive 30 day period, then all rights would automatically revert to the composers and the publisher would no longer have access to the composers work, registered on the blockchain. To set this smart contract in motion, both the composer and publisher and perhaps representatives of the publisher's finance and legal teams would sign using their private keys."

Smart contracts transactions that can only be approved by a large number of individuals are enforcing a "multiple signature protocol."

The two also elaborate a different use case, stating that "*A smart contract also provides a means for owners of assets to pool their resources and create a corporation on the blockchain where the articles of corporation are coded into the contract. Clearly spelling out and enforcing the rights of those owners. Associated agency contracts could define the decision rights of managers, encoding what they could and couldn't do with corporate resources without ownership permission."*

Smart contracts, in the context of Blockchain, dismiss concerns and fears about vote rigging or voter irregularities. They provide a very secure structure for any election process where you have votes that are ledger protected which will require both a large amount of computing power and decoding mechanisms for hackers to gain access.

Voter turnout also increases through smart contracts as voter apathy reduces. A lot of discouragement in the election process comes from the long queues and tedious identification verification processes that are common with traditional elections. We will examine several Blockchain-based elections in Part 3.

The immutable nature of data in the Blockchain means that any smart contract and its entire history is permanently embedded into the chain. Any outside interference and manipulation would need to overwhelm the consensus majority, and even then it would be openly visible to all participants in the network. These contracts are also verifiable on a case-by-case basis, the failure of one particular contract does not corrupt the integrity of the Blockchain itself.

We have so far uncovered a cryptographically encrypted peer-to-peer network that can transact freely and securely in itself wherein the only executing parties are the autonomously enforced contracts deployed by its users. We know how the information and smart contracts are stored inside the Merkle Trees inside blocks and how these blocks are linked together. We will examine the creation of new blocks and the way that this information is recorded next. It is arguably what gives Blockchain its groundbreaking potential.

Consensus Mechanisms

As a public database, it is essential that the information stored on the blockchain is honest and accurate. The process in which the data is recorded onto the chain epitomizes it's most revolutionary quality: decentralization. Consensus protocols are the third revolutionary aspect of Blockchain technology. The third pillar.

The terminology defines itself really; it is a particular means by which a mutual agreement of a data point and the state can be guaranteed. Rather than relying on a central authority to securely transact with other users, Blockchains utilize these innovative mechanisms across the network, to validate transactions and record data in a manner that is incorruptible. These mechanisms are responsible for the communication of data between nodes. They manifest the governing rules for agreement about how consensus is achieved in the network and what data is deemed legitimate and recorded in the next block.

These mechanisms aggregate millions of scattered, distributed devices together in a beautiful, incorruptible way of agreement, while also preventing exploitation of the system.

As a term, 'consensus' means that the nodes on the network agree on the state of a Blockchain, in a sense making it a self-auditing ecosystem. The mechanisms generally provide two essential functions.

Firstly, they enable the expansion of a blockchain, while ensuring that every new block is true. To achieve this, nodes participating in the consensus will 'Confirm Transactions' and 'Generate New Blocks' to arrange them in the chain.

Secondly, it provides a way to incentivize participants with rewards. These rewards come in the form of cryptocurrencies or tokens, which can be exceptionally lucrative, so much so that competition to confirm the next block in a chain is extremely fierce. The current reward for mining a new block in the Bitcoin network is 12.5 BTC.

Additionally, they prevent any single entity from controlling or derailing the whole Blockchain system. The aim of consensus rules is to guarantee a single chain is used and followed.

Consensus rules work as a code of conduct or as governing instructions for all nodes in the network. They are a specific set of rules that ensure that only a single block is created when validating transactions within it. The key requirement to achieve a consensus is a unanimous acceptance between nodes on the network for a single data value, even in the event of some of the nodes failing or being unreliable in any way.

As Blockchain technology does not rely on a central authority for security, every chain must have a way of securing itself against attacks. These protocols are designed to be difficult to imitate or replicate by being extremely costly to carry out, in terms of time, the computing resources required, or the holdings of a particular cryptocurrency.

With automated contracts, the fees that are usually collected by intermediary organizations are no longer a factor. Transacting on the Blockchain is drastically cheaper, as the only costs incurred by the parties involved are the nominal fees used to reward the miners or forgers that helped confirm your transaction.

The list of consensus mechanisms is ever-expanding, and it is not essential to our purpose in these pages to explore them all, we will inspect enough instances, however, to develop a firm grasp of the underlying concepts. The methods of consensus vary depending on the Blockchain, with a consistent ongoing debate as to what is the most effective and efficient protocol. We will explore Proof-of-Work and Proof-of-Stake in particular while brushing up on other mechanisms.

A typical real-world example of a consensus in this regard involves students in a particular class writing an examination. If the mechanism is applied in this scenario, all submitted scripts by all students in the class are completely identical. In the world of Blockchain, this type of consensus is perfect as it guarantees that every player involved in the network received an identical copy of the ledger. It must be noted that varying Consensus Mechanisms affect the security as well as the economic infrastructure of the cryptographic protocol in a variety of ways.

Continuing with our previous manner of dissecting complex concepts into their individual components, we will discuss a fundamental mathematical function of the most common consensus protocol at this time. Hashcash in the PoW algorithm.

Adam Back invented **Hashcash** in 1997 as a means to combat spam emails. It was used to attach a stamp to an email that took a quantifiable amount of work to compute. The stamp added a micro-cost to sending an email. This does not affect the average user, who may send a couple dozen emails in a day. But a spammer who sends fishing emails to lists that are millions of entries long is confronted with a considerable cost.

In Blockchain, Hashcash is a 'mathematical puzzle' that miners have to solve in quicktime to create a new block in the chain and then confirm the transaction between users. The first node to do so will be rewarded. The complexity of this mathematical problem is dependent on several factors that include; the total number of users, the existing power, and also the current load in the network. These variables are included in the equation to achieve an average, predefined block time. Hashcash is also a denial-of-service countermeasure technique.

The '**Proof-of-Work**' protocol is considered the original and first ever consensus algorithm in the space. It is a concept first invented by Cynthia Dwork and Moni Naor in 1993 and first formalized and coined in 1999 in a paper by Markus Jakobsson and Ari Juels. It was developed as an economic measure to deter certain digital abuses like spam transactions and DoS attacks by requiring some investment by the service requester. Utilizing a similar concept to

Hashcash, the PoW protocol requires some processing time by a computer before enabling an action. Limiting the number of requests a single node can make however opening up the network to 51% attacks.

The only way that new coins can be generated is for the executors of the PoW consensus algorithmic process to compete amongst themselves to execute and confirm transactions on the network in return for a reward. It is the only way in which the supply of coins can be increased and has been referred to as mining in the same way that mining is the only way to increase the supply of gold.

This is the process utilized by many cryptocurrencies as a means of minting new coins at a predefined inflation rate. A set quantity of coins is issued to the first node that solves the PoW process. This set quantity is known as the block subsidy, on top of which the node also receives the transaction fees paid by the senders of transactions. The two, the block subsidy and the transaction fees, make up the **Block Reward**. They are incentives for the people mining transactions and securing the chain. Bitcoin was the first cryptocurrency to make use of PoW consensus, which would evolve to form the basic standard that other cryptocurrencies would eventually adopt.

In the Bitcoin network, it takes a miner about 10 minutes to form a new block, as has been coded into the Genesis Block 0. The current block reward is 12.5 BTC. Other cryptocurrencies similar to Bitcoin like Litecoin also makes use of the PoW consensus algorithm, they differ slightly however. Litecoin's block time is 2.5 minutes, while the current block reward is 25 LTC. The Ethereum Blockchain currently still utilizes PoW and most projects powered by it make use of the same algorithm. PoW is the most commonly used consensus mechanism at this time.

As we discuss some of the significant advantages and disadvantages of the algorithm, it is important to differentiate between the effect of the mining hardware itself and of a network utilizing PoW. One of the major benefits of the Proof-of-Work algorithm is the implementation of constraints and limitations on specific actions on the network. Denial-of-Service attacks are spam attacks that have flooded major bank networks and systems like Bank of America, JPMorgan Chase, Wells Fargo, U.S. Bank, PNC Bank, and countless others. DoS attacks require a tremendous amount of computational power as well as time for calculations to be done. While DoS attacks are a threat to decentralized infrastructure, they are rarely worth the effort as they are incredibly expensive to execute.

Another benefit of utilizing computational power from hardware is that no specified amount of cryptocurrency is required in your digital wallet to confirm transactions and create new blocks. The PoW protocol transforms a world in which cash rules, into one where computational power has the upper hand. Any individual that can get their hands on a miner or mining capable GPU, for some networks, can start confirming transactions.

Operating a miner, however, can be a costly venture to pertain in. The mining process requires the use of specialized and highly advanced computer hardware. This hardware requires a lot of energy to function which further raises the operating cost. While you are not required to have a large balance to operate as a miner, you do need to make some heavy upfront capital investments. The high cost of mining has resulted in groups of individuals and organizations collaborating in mining pools in an effort to accumulate computational power and reduce upfront cost.

With the amount of money spent on acquiring specialized and advanced computer hardware as well as on vast amounts of electricity, you would think that miners' massive computational powers can be applied somewhere else other than to confirm transactions and create new blocks in a Blockchain network.

This is not the case as the hardware is specialized for this one application exclusively. The computational power cannot be used elsewhere. Advanced hardware with the sole purpose of calculating a specific hash algorithm, like the SHA-256, is referred to as an 'Application-Specific Integrated Circuit.' ASIC. While miners help to secure and sustain a Blockchain network, they are practically useless in other fields such as science and business.

The application executed by the network, however, can easily target scientific fields. The range of application of the mining hardware does not express the nearly limitless range of application of the network itself. The Golem network is a global, open-source supercomputer that utilizes combined computing power from users' machines. The computational power can be accessed by anyone. Altumea is another project enabling owners of modern graphic cards to sell idle computing power to buyers via micro-payments. This is a viable solution to monetize idle hardware and machines. It's cloud computing on steroids. Filecoin is a decentralized file storage network that brings together massive amounts of storage from "miners" all over the world and provides superior service with strong guarantees of availability, resilience, and great prices.

While PoW consensus has noteworthy benefits, it also has some obvious disadvantages. One vulnerability of PoW secured networks is '**51% attacks**' where an individual-miner or group of miners are in complete control of the majority of computational power. The attackers acquire majority control of the actions taking place on the network.

The creation of new blocks is monopolized, and most of the block reward goes to the attackers as they inhibit other miners from participating in the consensus and earning rewards in the process.

Majority or 51% attackers are also capable of reversing transactions. Miners tend to join a created branch in the Blockchain to leverage on the mining prowess of the branch, this branch could eventually become a majority and have more blocks than others.

51% attacks are not a really profitable venture as they require a humongous amount of computational and electrical power to execute. What's more, as soon as the public gets wind of what is going on, the network will be deemed to have been compromised which will eventually lead to users taking countermeasures or leaving the network and as a result, the value of the digital asset or cryptocurrency can significantly depreciate or appreciate in value and worth. Depending on whether the compromise deemed fatal or if the network prevailed and stands securer now than before.

We previously mentioned the difficulty target and nonce included in the PoW governed network's block header.

The target required is represented as the difficulty, where a higher difficulty represents a lower target. The **Difficulty** is manifested by the hash of the block header being required to be numerically lower than a certain target. The target is the number of zeroes that must be found when hashing the block header.

Depending on the network, the target is reset at a predetermined interval. It is written in the Genesis Block of Bitcoin that the difficulty target is reset every 2016 blocks by up to a factor four up or down. Hereby the difficulty is adjusted that the average hashrate available in the last 2016 blocks would take about 14 days to mine 2016 blocks, which is about ten minutes per block. If due to an increase in hashing power, it takes only ten days to mine 2016 blocks, the difficulty is increased by a factor of 1.4.

The **Nonce** is the value that is altered by the miners to try different permutations to achieve the difficulty level required. The nonce in a bitcoin block is a 32-bit (4-byte) numeric whose value is adjusted so that the hash of the block will be less than or equal to the current target of the network.

As part of the block data, any change to the nonce will make the block hash completely different. Every time a new block candidate is hashed, the result is completely unpredictable, so eventually, one block candidate will fulfill the difficulty requirement. When this happens, the successful miner broadcasts the new block to the network. Since it is believed infeasible to predict which combination of bits will result in the right hash, many different nonce values are tried, and the hash is recomputed for each value until a hash less than or equal to the current target of the network is found. As this iterative calculation requires time and resources, the presentation of the block with the correct nonce value constitutes Proof-of-Work.

Every other node in the network will also make sure that the block is actually valid. This includes testing the validity of the block hash from the header, as well as checking every single transaction.

An interesting nugget of knowledge. The first transaction of every block is a unique type of transaction that can only be created by a miner. It has no inputs, and there is one created with each new block. It is called the 'coinbase' transaction and includes the recipient or recipients of the block reward and the transaction fees. It also includes the nonce and other block specific data.

Due to the very high computing energy needed to solve hash problems involved in Proof-of-Work, it is becoming more centralized rather than the initial idea of it being decentralized causing miners to convert larger shares of winning blocks to themselves.

Miners under the PoW system require a lot of electricity. The data in 2018 shows that around 4,3 million homes in the United States of America could be powered with the energy consumed by the Bitcoin network. It is responsible for about 0.2% of the worlds energy consumption. Recent 2018 studies detail that the mining of Bitcoin blocks used more energy than the Scandinavian country of Denmark.

Now the cost of using all this electricity is paid in full with Fiat currencies such as USD ($), Euro (€) or GBP (£); this adds pressure on the cryptocurrencies as it depreciates in its trading value and worth. The Ethereum Blockchain ecosystem has therefore decided to explore the use of the PoS algorithm as a viable alternative to PoW.

'**Proof-of-Stake**' takes a different approach. Rather than using computational power to decide who confirms a block, the nodes in a PoS governed network that create new blocks are selected based on their overall stake or wealth. In a PoW system, a miner gets rewarded for solving puzzles and creating new blocks, in the Proof-of-Stake consensus mechanism there is no block reward, all that is given to the selected nodes are the transaction fees. These nodes in a PoS system are aptly referred to as 'forgers.'

While the concept of Proof-of-Stake was first mentioned on a forum hosted by Bitcoin in 2011, the first actual use of this mechanism was back in 2012 by a cryptocurrency known as Peercoin.

In a typical PoS consensus, you are unlikely to create a block in the network, as a holder of a small cryptocurrency balance. This is similar to miners not being able to engage in the mining of a block in the network because the miners have a low hashrate.

A user with a small cryptocurrency balance may spend a long time without being able to create a block, the operation as a forger requires nodes to hold a significant balance which invariably means that only a few holders eventually qualify and end up monopolizing the creation of blocks.
For the best form of security on the Blockchain network, it is better if there are more people participating in this process. It is therefore vital to incentivize the system so that holders of small balances can also actively participate.

The PoS algorithm comes in two variants which are often used rather than the typical PoS in its raw, original, and true form. These variants are DPoS (Delegated Proof-of-Stake) and LPoS (Leased Proof-of-Stake) and have their respective benefits when utilized.

With '**Leased Proof-of-Stake**' (LPoS), holders are allowed to lease out their corresponding crypto balances to a staking node or forger. The holder of the digital assets that are leased out will still be in complete control of their funds, and they can transfer or spend the funds freely, of course, the lease agreement invariably comes to an end if the funds are spent. Thus is the beauty of smart contracts. Very similar to the example of a composer deploying a smart contract to a publisher that we discussed previously. The leased out cryptocurrency boosts the chances of the staking node creating a block in the network. Rewards that are received for the creation are proportionally shared between the lease and the leaser.

In '**Delegated Proof-of-Stake**' (DPoS), holders of cryptocurrency make use of their respective balances to vote for a number of nodes or forgers that will be given the chance to create new blocks on the chain. In a DPoS consensus governed system every crypto holder is fully engaged, however, they may not necessarily be directly rewarded in the same manner as in the Leased Proof-of-Stake approach. The balance holders, however, are allowed to vote on any changes to the network parameters which gives them a sense of ownership.

Dan Larimer proposed a system in which people in the network vote for 'witnesses' that have a responsibility to secure the network, each of which is to put some amount of digital currency in escrow. Since the witnesses have funds in escrow, it gives them a good incentive to act in accordance with the system. Any witness caught acting maliciously is voted out and replaced with an already awaiting witness and also relieved of the funds they had in escrow.

This way, the Blockchain network security is maintained. Examples of Delegated Proof-of-Stakes Blockchains are STEEM and EOS. DPoS critics claim that the protocol does not favor those with smaller funds or the small players.

Proof-of-Stake is believed to be a more cost effective and less energy consuming consensus mechanism. As mentioned before, the reward systems for both PoW and PoS are different. In a Proof-of-Work system, it is possible that the miner has no stake in the cryptocurrency that is being mined. A forger, however, is required to own a stake in the processed cryptocurrency. A forger always owns the digital assets involved in the process or acquires it through a leasing agreement as in the case of the Leased Proof-of-Stake. Ethereum will be moving to DPoS with its Casper project.

The '**Proof-of-Elapsed Time**' (PoET) consensus mechanism is generally utilized on 'permissioned blockchains,' this means that every node in the network must be wholly identifiable and must have been fully permitted to operate. Also referred to as private or closed Blockchains. In a network in which all nodes are identifiable and less competition exists, networks can choose more efficient and cost-effective solutions.

To better understand what the Proof-of-Elapsed Time is all about, imagine a class of 20 students writing an exam and there's a big old wall clock in front of the class. The wall clock is set to coincide with the duration of the examination and the time left for the submission of the paper is 30 minutes.

After 30 minutes all 20 students submit their scripts and wait to receive their next task. The key being that each of the students receives a random and different amount of time they need to wait before being able to complete their next task. Within the PoET mechanism, each node has a separate 'time-to-wait' that is assigned to them at random by the network.

Once the time-to-wait has elapsed, the node can then create a new block on the chain. In PoET the node with the shortest amount of time is better off. In a real-world scenario it is a case of drawing straws, only, in this case, the person that draws the shortest straw takes priority over the individuals that draw the longer ones.

Intel created the Proof-of-Elapsed Time consensus mechanism in 2016. It is utilized by Hyperledger Sawtooth which is a platform capable of building, implementing, and operating distributed ledgers. Proof-of-Elapsed Time conserves energy better than the Proof-of-Stake as each of the nodes has a different 'time-to-wait' and are not all competing against each other. The direct competition between nodes is fairer as there are fewer participants.

PoI is an acronym for '**Proof-of-Importance**,' which is a consensus mechanism that was first deployed by NEO which is a protocol platform. In PoI, your currency balance is only one of the determining factors in the staking of a block of transactions on the network. The nodes stand a clear chance of creating blocks on the chain based on several factors that include; the asset balance, the reputation of the node based on a different mechanism, and the volume of transactions to and from the address. These factors determine the 'usefulness' of nodes in the network.

We now have a firm grasp of how Blockchain stores data and assets and how these are transacted directly and freely. Before concluding this informative section of the book, we will indulge in some interesting pieces of information.

Alan Turing invented the Universal Turing Machine in 1936 after he defined it in his highly influential publication, *On Computable Numbers, with an application to the Entscheidungsproblem.*

Previously do that, Alan had developed several different Turing machines, which were application specific automatic machines, each corresponding to a different program or algorithm.

Turing machines embodied the algorithm, while the Universal Turing Machine could be turned to any well-defined task by being supplied with the algorithm.

Turing Completeness on a Blockchain refers to the ability of the network to exercise functions for memory and data changes and if/else statements. It really refers to the ability to code programmable smart contracts onto a Blockchain. Compared to the Ethereum Blockchain, the Bitcoin Blockchain is not Turing complete as it has almost zero ability for data manipulation. Blockchains can add said functionality through network-wide updates in the protocol. Bitcoin intends to add some Smart Contract functionality.

While large parts of the Blockchain infrastructure are designed to reduce the role of intermediaries, that does not mean that the technology is not perfectly capable of cooperating with third-parties.

Blockchains cannot access data outside their network. To be able to use external factors as conditions and triggers of a smart contract, a third-party agent is required. An **Oracle** provides the values that trigger an event to the smart contract in a secure and trusted manner. It finds and verifies real-world occurrences and submits this information to the Blockchain. It is a data feed that provides external data, such as the weather temperature, successful payments, price fluctuations, etc.

Oracles are part of multi-signature contracts where, for example, the original trustees sign a contract for future release of funds only if certain conditions are met. Before any funds get released an oracle has to sign the smart contract as well.

Stuart Haber and W. Scott Stornetta developed a time-stamped series of records in 1991 intent on developing a computationally practical procedure for digital record keeping.

It was Nick Szabo, a legal scholar, and cryptographer, that first proposed and coined the term Smart Contracts, back in 1994.

The predecessor to the first ever consensus algorithm was invented by Cynthia Dwork and Moni Naor in 1993. Adam Back developed Hashcash in 1997 as a means to combat spam emails and Markus Jakobsson and Ari Juels formalized and coined the marriage of Dwork's, Naor's, and Back's work 'Proof-of-Work' in 1999.

Yet years would pass in anticipation of a visionary mind that would merge these seemingly foreign concepts together into a technological Rembrandt.

Satoshi Nakamoto released the official Bitcoin whitepaper in October 2008. It showcased Satoshi's vision of a truly global peer-to-peer digital currency and detailed the beautiful marriage of Blockchain, Proof-of-Work, and Smart Contracts. This symbiosis, for the first time, offered a viable solution to the Double-Spending obstacle which had plagued computer scientists in the years between. Bitcoin accomplished this without having to rely on a centralized server or trusted institution.

A quick note, '**whitepaper**' is a recycled term from the early 20th century and has found a solid standing in the cryptocurrency world as a document that explains and promotes the product or service of a specific company or project. It is often used as a marketing tool and has evolved into the fundamental backbone of many of today's Blockchain projects and companies.

It is interesting to note that in the original whitepaper developed by Satoshi Nakamoto, he never referred to the distributed ledger as a blockchain, but with two separate words, namely; "block" and "chain."

While it is a dry read, you can take a look at the Bitcoin white paper here: https://bitcoin.org/bitcoin.pdf

The Nakamoto institute is an excellent resource for all on-line communications and posts from and relating to Satoshi. https://satoshi.nakamotoinstitute.org

With Blockchain, two individuals can engage in a transaction involving an exchange of services or goods for cryptocurrency without the need for supervision by a third-party which will significantly reduce counter-party risk. It transforms the way industries operate on a fundamental level, by ensuring that users are in complete control of all information as well as every transaction. Power is truly in the hands of users. The data in a Blockchain network is reputed as being complete, precise, consistent, timely, and widely accessible.

The decentralized infrastructure of the technology means that there is less risk from a centralized point of attack and of failure. To this end, Blockchain networks are capable of handling mischievous cyber-attacks much better than centralized networks.

Public Blockchains are transparent since any change to the Blockchain can be viewed by any concerned party. Every transaction is immutable, and every change in the protocol is publicly visible. Additionally, all transactions are added to a single public ledger which drastically minimizes the complexities as well as clutter that is experienced with multiple ledgers, providing an efficiently streamlined ecosystem.

With trusted third-party involvement redundant in a Blockchain network, the cost of trading and exchanging assets is significantly reduced. Traditional banks, Mastercard, Visa, and PayPal, act as a third-party for transactions between people or corporate entities. With a trustless system, copies of the ledger are given to everyone involved in the transaction removing the need for any of the parties to put their trust in a third-party to set up a transaction as the parties can easily authenticate all of the written information directly.

With a fully automated, transparent, and accurate Blockchain structure, you reduce any breakdown in workflow or communication by limiting discrepancies associated with independent styled processing. Thus dramatically enhancing the efficiency of management and accounting processes.

The transfer of value on a global scale is quick with regards to Blockchain because there is no need for intermediaries to be in place to help with dispute resolution as is the case with other centralized networks.

Bitcoin-related transactions cannot be reversed, and they are essentially final in every respect. Which means there is no need for sender and recipient bank to validate your transaction for you.

While Interbank based transactions involve the process of clearing and settling which can take a number of days to accomplish, in addition to having to reestablished trust for each new transaction. With blockchain-based transactions, processing times are reduced to a matter of seconds and minutes. Efficiently, there are no business days in the Blockchain world. There is only block time or other means of transaction consensus. Blockchain processing is not done from "9 to 5," but for "24/7," and "365 days" in a year.

Smart contracts reduce the likelihood of supply chains being affected by issues associated with traditional systems where various forms are passed around for approval and thereby increasing the potential for failures in the process. Blockchain provides a fully accessible and secure virtual/ digital alternative for every participant in the supply chain with the various tasks as well as payments fully automated.

It is likely that in the future smart contracts will offer fully automated systems to aid the detection of culprits in a car accident. Smart contracts could also be advantageous in the provision of mechanisms for driverless cars and will enable auto insurance companies to provide more efficient and reliable insurance packages. They also allow the sensors in your car to communicate with the sensors in the cars around it. Purchasing and selling data as an AI seems fit. Your car could purchase live camera footage from the vehicles in front and behind you to expand the vision of its' own sensors.

Real estate transactions are far more fluid when a smart contract is coded to automatically transfer the ownership of a property to the buyer's address when the correct amount of value has been received by the seller's address. You can sell your property efficiently and anonymously without the need for brokers and notaries.

It is also viable to store and encode private health data in a Blockchain structure. The specific nodes authorized to have access to the health data would be required to utilize a private key.

The creation of this technology that is gradually, but surely changing the world is still shrouded in mystery. No one is sure if Satoshi Nakamoto is actually the name of the individual that conceptualized the much-heralded Blockchain technology or just a pseudonym adopted by a group of anonymous geeky inventors, or even a secret government institution.

We have so far uncovered the functions and composition of some of the fundamental concepts of Blockchain technology. In detail, we have inspected the manner in which Blockchain is utilized in the storage and security of data, while Smart Contracts facilitate the exchange, and Consensus Mechanisms are responsible for the recording. Different cryptographic systems are responsible for the privatization and anonymization of the data, and a peer-to-peer network serves as the foundation for the infrastructure.

"I think the internet is going to be one of the major forces for reducing the role of government. The one thing that's missing but that will soon be developed, is a reliable e-cash."

Milton Friedman

(in 1999)

Part 2

A Technological Odyssey

In the previous part, we discussed the technologies that make up Blockchain, how they function, and what they provide.

We will discuss specific concepts like the Byzantine Generals Problem and Double Spending in the context of an accurate recollection of historical milestones of the technology, next. Examining achievements, discoveries, and breakthroughs along the way. We will overcome challenges, face obstacles, suffer devastating blows, and battle giants.

We will reestablish the importance of the core values that distributed and decentralized technology provides to its users. Some of which are rooted in one particular aspect of Blockchain, whereas others are a result of a blend of facets of the technology.

Digital currencies seem like a logical progression from the advent of the internet, why have they taken so long to find a solid footing?

There are different technological challenges that had to be overcome.

The '**Byzantine Generals' Problem**' details a story about a group of Byzantine generals surrounding a city which they intended to conquer. In order to successfully do so, they all have to attack at once and in synchrony. The attack only has a chance of success if all generals participate. A single corrupt general or false message means utter defeat. The generals can only communicate through messengers, delivering notes on foot, with no way of validating the authenticity and origin of any message.

There are several problems faced in this scenario. Any of the messengers could be captured, and the message would not be delivered, and because of that, a synchronized attack would be impossible. Furthermore, the generals couldn't be sure if any of the other generals were traitors intending to send false messages as a means of purposely sabotaging the attack.

A dishonest general could tell half of the generals that the plan is to retreat, ensuring that they do so, while telling the other half to attack, dooming them to failure. Anyone of these scenarios can be referred to as a Byzantine Failure.

Where there is a '**Byzantine Failure**' in a distributed computing system, the problematic components may show up as both functioning and failed to the failure-detection mechanisms. In this situation, the failed components of the distributed computing system will appear differently to different people observing it. To some, it will appear as being in perfect working condition while to others it will look as being faulty.

This makes it hard for the other fully functional components to isolate the failure from the network since a consensus has to be reached, but with observers having conflicting outcomes it becomes increasingly problematic.

The story transfers and applies to nodes attempting to agree on the information that they are displaying across the peer-to-peer network, stating that no two computers on a decentralized network can entirely and irrefutably guarantee that they are displaying the same data. Assuming the network is unreliable, they can never be sure that the data that they communicated has arrived.

Byzantine Fault Tolerance is a way of overcoming this challenging situation. At its core, BFT is about achieving a consensus across a distributed network of devices, some of which could be potentially faulty, while also being wary of any attackers attempting to undermine the network.
Achieving Byzantine Fault Tolerance is one of the most difficult challenges addressed by Blockchain technology. It

refers to the ability of two nodes communicating safely across a network, knowing that they are displaying the same data.

It is all about finding out how dependable or reliable distributed computing systems that have been originally built to be fault-tolerant really are. This is particularly significant in a situation where some components of the systems fail or act maliciously.

With a Consensus Mechanism applied in this scenario, the camps have an agreement on the chain of messages sent and received and each camp can have confidence knowing that they are all on the same page. These general consensus agreements ensure that the network is Byzantine Fault Tolerant.

Byzantine Fault Tolerance aims to protect distributed computing systems from component failures whether or not there are symptoms that will stop the other components of the system from coming to a unanimous consensus or agreement. A consensus is required in order to rectify the faulty component and ensure the proper functioning of the network.

It refers to the networks ability to secure and safeguard the Blockchain. In simple terms, the network needs to be able to counteract 'harmful' nodes and come to an agreement on the right and current state of the Blockchain.

The Byzantine Generals' Problem is rarely the first challenge people imagine that Blockchain technology faced. However, safe and reliable communication between nodes is a considerable problem and an incredible achievement that it has been resolved, allowing for consensus to be reached between the nodes on the network.

There are different approaches taken by different consensus protocols in order to arrive at a secure and efficient consensus, as we have discussed in Part 1.

The infamous '**Double-Spending**' is an attack that takes advantage of a technological design flaw, in which a particular set of cryptocurrencies are spent in more than a single transaction. It has been the main obstacle for cryptographers and computer scientists in recent history, next to BFT and network consensus, and refers to a flaw exclusive to digital tokens. It exploits the ability to duplicate a token as it consists of digital files that can be modified, copied, and pasted just like any other file on your computer. Double-spending causes inflation and falsifies the currency just like counterfeit money does to our existing fiat currencies.

In addition to devaluing the currency through inflation, it also diminishes the users trust in the digital asset. Several solutions to double-spending have been proposed, until recent history, the majority of which resorted to utilizing a centralized third-party that verifies the token economics, whether the balance is high enough and that it has appropriately been spent. Think PayPal. PayPal is a trusted intermediary between sender and recipient or buyer and seller that verifies that the sender has enough 'balance' to send a transaction and also that the exact balance is removed from the sender's account and added to the recipient's. While this system works, it represents a single point of failure and trust in the transaction. Additionally, these intermediaries like to charge a fee to provide this service.

Double spending can occur in the following ways;

1. **The Race Attack:** This is where a couple of conflicting transactions are sent in quick succession to the network.

2. **The Finney Attack:** This is when a user pre-mines a single transaction to a block and then spends the same cryptocurrencies prior to the release of the block in order to make the transaction invalid.

3. **A 51% Attack:** This is where a user reverses whatever transaction they want by owning 51% or more of the overall computing power in the network. This user also has complete control of all the transaction data in the generated blocks in the chain.

1. To take care of the Race Attack Double-Spend issue and prevent any damage that could occur; as a result, one has to wait for each transaction to be validated, in other words, a single confirmation must appear on a particular transaction.

2. The Finney Attack, named after Hal Finney a cryptographic activist and developer, can be prevented when you wait for a total of six confirmations to occur on a single transaction where the transaction is quite big. If the transaction is a small one, then you have to wait till a minimum of just one confirmation appears on the transaction.

3. 51% Attacks can have a very devastating effect on the whole network. They require a tremendous amount of investment in both computing power and energy to achieve. The reward consists of the native currency of the network, which depreciates corresponding to the success of the attack, lowering the value of the annexed value. It is not lucrative in the end and a major reason why 51% attacks are a rarity.

Byzantine Generals' Problem and Double-Spending were arguably the two largest obstacles in Blockchain's path. Technological challenges that took decades to overcome. Yet, brilliant minds and visionaries have theorized the advancements long ago.

How far we've come

The history of Blockchain is not only fascinating but tells a story of international collaboration combined with individual brilliance.

We can trace the origins of Blockchain back until **1982**. The year in which David Chaum, a computer scientist, proposed the concept of e-Cash. He detailed an innovative form of cryptography in his paper, *Blind signatures for untraceable payments.* The system would enable automatic payments without third-party access to the transaction data.

Chaums dedication to privacy in the digital realm grew until he created DigiCash in **1989**. DigiCash would create a blind signature system to enable a safe, secure, online currency. It was a distinguished predecessor of the digital currencies of today and a crucial early proponent of public and private key cryptography. DigiCash transactions were unique in that they were anonymous due to a number of cryptographic protocols developed by Chaum.

While DigiCash enjoyed several years of operation, it never broke into the mainstream to the degree that it's developers intended. The product itself never caught on, and the company declared bankruptcy in 1998 and subsequently sold its assets to eCash Technologies, another digital currency company.

In **1991**, Stuart Haber and W. Scott Stornetta provided research work for a chain of records that are secured cryptographically. The procedure removes the need for any third-party validation or record-keeping service while maintaining complete privacy of the documents themselves so that it is infeasible for a user either to back-date or to forward-date his document, even with the collusion of a time-stamping service.

Two years later, in **1993** Cynthia Dwork and Moni Naor developed a protocol against spam transactions and DoS attacks. The procedure would require some form of economic investment by the requested.

It was a year later in **1994** when Nick Szabo proposed digital agreements between parties that are trackable and irreversible and allow the conduction and performance of credible transactions without any third-party.

In **1997**, Adam Back invented hashcash. The algorithm was implemented as a Denial-of-Service countermeasure technique in a number of systems.

Four years after the proposition of Smart Contracts, in **1998**, Szabo designed the mechanism for 'Bit Gold,' a decentralized digital currency. Szabo's reasoning for alternative currency was to create something that did not require a third-party, like a central bank, to create or manage it.

During the same year, Wei Dai released an essay detailing his idea for 'b-money,' a cryptocurrency whose exchange reads similarly to what the Blockchain in Bitcoin would eventually become. The proof-of-work system creates the currency by solving a mathematical computation, and the transfer of money is broadcasted to the network.

Neither of these proposals, however, came to fruition.

Although the Bit Gold project was never implemented, it has since been called, "*a direct precursor to the Bitcoin architecture.*" There are undeniable similarities between Bitcoin's architecture and the Bit gold proposal, particularly in the PoW governed consensus mechanism.

A year later, in **1999**, the protocol invented by Cynthia Dwork and Moni Naor, was formalized and coined Proof-of-Work in a paper by Markus Jakobsson and Ari Juels.

The main challenges for digital currencies had by now been overcome. Separately and independently, different minds had pushed the boundaries of computer science and cryptography into new terrains. Now we needed someone with a vision to put the disparate technological puzzle pieces together.

The year **2008** saw the birth of the myth of Satoshi Nakamoto. He/she or they commenced work on the concept of Bitcoin in Japan. Online communication about technologically relevant topics begins here. His first email starting with the now infamous words:

"I've been working on a new electronic cash system that's fully peer-to-peer, with no trusted third-party."

From here on over the next couple years, Blockchain's history is indistinguishable from Bitcoin's history.

Vladimir Oksman, Charles Bry, and Neal Kin registered the Bitcoin website (www.bitcoin.org) in **August 2008** via anonymousspeech.com, a website where domain names can be purchased anonymously. The three individuals also filed an encryption patent application together, but have all since denied having any link to Satoshi Nakamoto.

Nakamoto released the official Bitcoin whitepaper in **October 2008,** which showcased Satoshi's vision of a truly global peer-to-peer digital currency. He was able to provide a viable solution for the issues plaguing extant and historical examples of digital currency by combining some of the major technological breakthroughs of the past two and a half decades, namely Blockchain, Smart Contracts, and Consensus Mechanisms. Nakamoto provided the basis for the legitimization of decentralized currency.

Whatever the case may be, Blockchain was created to act as the public transaction ledger for the world's first digital asset that provided viable solutions for the existent challenges surrounding the evolution of the technology, Bitcoin.

With the marriage of Blockchain, Proof-of-Work, and Smart Contracts for Bitcoin, the issue of Double-Spending had been effectively resolved without having to rely on a centralized server or trusted institution.

A completely decentralized payment system. Nakamoto detailed the main properties of his peer-to-peer currency in an email.

"The main properties:
Double-spending is prevented with a peer-to-peer network.
No mint or other trusted parties.
Participants can be anonymous.
New coins are made from Hashcash style proof-of-work.
The proof-of-work for new coin generation also powers the

network to prevent double-spending."

A brief explanation of an intensely powerful and radical technology.

Three months later on **January 3rd** of **2009**, the first block of Bitcoin, known as the Genesis block, was mined, symbolizing a radical change and transformation of many existing narratives surrounding governments and social infrastructure. It will likely remain an important milestone in human history throughout the decades. By Jan. 9th, the first iteration of the Bitcoin software was released, three days later, the first-ever Bitcoin transaction occurred as Nakamoto sent 10 Bitcoins to infamous computer programmer Hal Finney.

Later that same year, in **October** of **2009**, the New Liberty Standard valued Bitcoin at 1 USD to 1,309 BTC. The cost of energy required to operate the distributed computing systems that generate Bitcoins was factored into the equation.

Two months later in **December**, Nakamoto released the second version of the software.

Two months into the next year, **February 2010**, the first ever Hong Kong Bitcoin Counter was made public, and the first global Bitcoin market was established by (dwdollar) which ironically is no longer in existence.

On **May 22**, **2010**, Laslo Hanyecz a programmer residing in Florida sent 10,000 BTC to a volunteer in the United Kingdom who ordered pizza for him from Papa John's spending $25 in the process. This infamous day would come to be known as 'Pizza Day,' manifesting the first real-world transaction with Bitcoin on a Blockchain.

Mt. Gox, a Bitcoin exchange based in Tokyo, Japan was launched in **July 2010**, by US programmer Jed McCaleb, who later went on to found Ripple. Rather interestingly, the name Mt. Gox stood for, *"Magic: The Gathering On-line eXchange."*

Just a month later, in **August**, a weakness in the way the network validates the value of Bitcoin was discovered and exploited. This led to a total of 92 billion Bitcoins being generated and the crash of the value of the cryptocurrency at the time.

Half a year later, in **February** of **2011** for the first time in its existence, the value of Bitcoin was at par with the USD. One BTC equaled one USD. By June of the same year however, the value of one Bitcoin would increase to $31.

Mt. Gox expanded rapidly to become by far the most popular Bitcoin exchange in the world after being purchased by French developer and Bitcoin enthusiast Mark Karpelés in **March 2011**.

2011 included the infamous exit of Nakamoto. In the years since he, she, or they disappeared into the ether and left the technology in the hands of a few high-profile developers, Nakamoto's words have become nigh-gospel for some in the Bitcoin world.

Nakamoto's online activity, messages, and emails range from 2009 all the way to 2011 when the anonymous creator sent their now-legendary goodbye note to Mike Hearn:

"I've moved on to other things. It's in good hands with Gavin [Andresen] and everyone."

Mt. Gox was hacked in **June 2011**, as a result of a compromised computer, belonging to an auditor of the company. The hacker used the authorized access to enter the exchange and artificially alter the nominal value of Bitcoin to one cent. He transferred around 2,000 Bitcoins from customer accounts before selling them. As a result of this hack, Mt. Gox took a number of security measures, including arranging for a substantial amount of its Bitcoin to be taken offline and held in cold storage.

Among notable moments for Bitcoin in **2012**, it crossed the $100 threshold in **April,** while the technology made steady progress throughout the year.

By **2013** and into **2014**, Mt. Gox was handling over 70% of all bitcoin transactions worldwide, as the largest Bitcoin intermediary and the world's leading Bitcoin exchange.

Bitcoin's price saw its share of ups and downs in **2013**, but it passed a value of $1,000 for the first time and was becoming the most recognizable and successful wallet and exchange available.

The market capitalization of Bitcoin reached 1 billion USD in **March 2013**. A guidance report for individuals utilizing, exchanging and administering cryptocurrencies such as Bitcoin was issued by the US Financial Crimes Enforcement Network or otherwise known as FINCEN.

In **June 2013,** the founder of a Bitcoin Forum reported the first Bitcoin theft; he had 25,000 BTC taken from his digital wallet, this amount had a real-world value of 375,000 USD at the time.

The testing of Bitcoin data on the Bloomberg terminal commenced in **August 2013**. With Bloomberg's endorsement, the reputation and legitimacy of Bitcoin was further enhanced. This led to a rise in the demand as people's confidence in the cryptocurrency grew.

Bitcoin was developed to achieve one goal: create a decentralized alternative to the existing financial industry. Vitalik Buterin, a cryptocurrency researcher and programmer, saw the potential for using Blockchain for other things and pushed for a scripting language for Bitcoin to make development of applications on the Blockchain possible but his proposal was rejected.

In late 2013, he proposed the development of a new platform with support for more generalized scripting and application development.
Ethereum is a platform built to enable developers to easily code and launch their own applications that run on all nodes in the Ethereum network without having to code their own Blockchain. Buterin published the Ethereum whitepaper describing the proposed technology in **November** of **2013**.

The Federal Reserve chairman in **2013** was Ben Bernanke, and he stated that *"Bitcoin may hold long-term promise, particularly if the innovations promote a faster, more secure and more efficient payment system."* This was in light of the price of Bitcoin rising to 700 USD. The US Senate also held its first-ever hearing on the cryptocurrency in **November**.

In **December** of **2013,** the central bank of China placed a ban on Bitcoin transactions by financial institutions in the country. The People's Bank of China further stated that Bitcoin was not a legal tender and cannot be bestowed the same legal status as is the case with Fiat currency. China banned Bitcoin because of the perceived risk to its capital control and financial stability. Today about 80% of the global transactions are processed right in China making the country the world's largest trader of Bitcoin.

Elliptic, Bitcoin custodians, launched the first-ever insured Bitcoin storage solution service tailored for their institutional clientele back in **January 2014**.

On **7th of February 2014**, Mt. Gox stopped all Bitcoin withdrawals, claiming that it was merely pausing withdrawal requests, *"to obtain a clear technical view of the currency process."* After a number of weeks of uncertainty, on **February 24th, 2014**, the exchange suspended all trading, and the website went offline.

During the same week, a leaked corporate document claimed that hackers had raided the exchange and stole

744,408 Bitcoins belonging to Mt. Gox customers, as well as an additional 100,000 belonging to the company.

On **February 28th,** Mt. Gox filed for bankruptcy protection in Japan, and two weeks later in the US.

In **April 2014**, the company began liquidation proceedings.

The New York State Department of Financial Services unveiled their first draft for the regulation of cryptocurrency in **July 2014**. Simultaneously, the European Banking Authority published their view on cryptocurrency, recommending that EU legislators treat cryptos as "obliged entities" and indicated that cryptocurrencies should be compliant with both anti-money laundering (AML) and the requirements for counter-terrorist financing.

The Ethereum team needed development funding to create the network and decided to reach out to the cryptocurrency community in a crowdsale. The crowdsale ran in July and **August 2014** and allowed future users and investors to purchase Ether, the native currency, in exchange for Bitcoin. Since Bitcoin was an established currency at the time, the Ethereum team could trade it in for fiat currency to cover development costs. During the crowdsale, 11.9 million Ether were sold, raising about 18.4 million USD.

At the end of the year, in **December 2014,** Microsoft started accepting payment for products and services in Bitcoin.

In **January** of **2015**, the New York Stock Exchange invested in the 75 million USD funding round of Coinbase. NYSE intended to bring confidence, transparency, and security to Bitcoin while capitalizing on this new class of assets.

The Ethereum system went live on **July 30th**, **2015**, with 72 million coins 'premined.'

The Hyperledger project was founded in **December 2015**, when the Linux Foundation announced a collaboration of a number of enterprise players, including IBM, Intel, Fujitsu, and JP Morgan. Hyperledger is an umbrella project of open-source Blockchains and related tools.

The goal was to improve and create industry collaboration around the technology so that it would be applicable for complex enterprise use cases in the key industries most suitable to Blockchain disruption: technology, finance, and supply chain.

The project gained substance in 2016 when the first technology donations were made. IBM donated what was to become known as Hyperledger Fabric, and Intel donated the code base that became Hyperledger Sawtooth.

Unlike most projects in the Blockchain space, Hyperledger has never issued its own cryptocurrency. In fact, the executive director of Hyperledger has publicly stated that there will never be one.

STEAM is a digital distribution network that engages in the sale of personal computer video games and other similar hardware. In **April 2016**, Steam started accepting payment in Bitcoin particularly from consumers residing in developing countries from around the world to avoid cross-border fee payments and pretty high-interest rates amongst other related charges.

The Decentralized Autonomous Organization, known as The DAO launched on **April 30th, 2016**. It raised over 100 million USD by May 15th, and by the end of the funding period, raised over 150 million USD, making it the largest crowdfunding in history.

It was a virtual venture capital fund that is governed by the investors of the DAO. It was built with smart contracts on the Ethereum Blockchain and without a central authority, which reduced costs and in theory provided more control and access to the investors.

On **June 17th, 2016**, a hacker found a loophole in the code that allowed him to drain funds from The DAO. He stole

70 million USD worth of ETH within the first hours, before voluntarily withdrawing from the attack. He had done the damage he intended. 3.6 million Ether were taken.

The hacker was able to 'ask' the smart contract to give the Ether back multiple times before the contract updated its balance. Two main issues made this possible: the fact that when the DAO smart contract was created the coders did not take the possibility of a recursive call into account and the fact that the smart contract first sent the ETH funds and then updated the internal token balance. The code written for The DAO had multiple flaws, and the recursive call exploit was one of them.

It is, however, important to remember that this flaw did no come from the Ethereum Blockchain, but from this one application that was built on it. Ethereum was not compromised.

With Britain deciding to leave the European Union in **June** of **2016**, Bitcoin witnessed a 9% rise in its value, while the value of the GBP simultaneously dropped by 8%.

Discussions about how to proceed with the Ethereum Blockchains started immediately following the exploit. It split the entire community amongst the people for a hard fork in which the Blockchain would be altered through a consensus or against to uphold the immutable and permanent nature of the Blockchain. The hard fork proposal was voted for and accepted by the majority of the Ethereum community. It completed on **July 20th,** and the funds were returned to the investors.

The Ethereum hard-fork did not, however, prevent all participants from following the old main branch and while the newly created branch remained Ethereum, the former branch continued on as Ethereum Classic.

Despite the expected unreasonable attitude of the Chinese authorities toward cryptocurrencies, they still invested in the technology. The country's digitalization strategy, identified in the 13th Five-Year Plan for National Informatization in **December 2016**, states:

"The Internet, cloud computing, large data, artificial intelligence, machine learning, blockchain… will drive the evolution of everything — digital, network and intelligent services will be everywhere."

The Bitcoin 'transaction volume' is a metric used to describe the volume of commodities purchased with Bitcoin and also the amount of Bitcoin that is stored up in digital wallet addresses. In **September 2016**, the Bitcoin transaction volume reached 100 billion USD. Even though a huge amount of Bitcoin is being saved or invested, the transaction volume is a good indicator that the currency is used in the buying and selling of commodities.

At the start of **2017**, Bitcoin was worth 1,100 USD. By the end of the year, the value would be fifteen times that much. Despite the rise in the value of Bitcoin, however, the network was strongly criticized by traditional stakeholders and financial analysts such as Jamie Dimon, who blatantly called people that invested in Bitcoin, "*stupid.*" Yet, even in the face of mounting criticism from mainstream investors and analysts, Bitcoin continued to soar in value.

The Ethereum Blockchain was established in 2015, but it was in **2017** when the network truly began to get noticed, and a considerable number of applications started using the Ethereum technology. At this present point in time, there are over 850 applications driven by Ethereum Blockchain. Many of these applications utilized it to create native currencies in their ecosystem which often followed Ethereum's manner of crowdfunding. Which would soon be coined 'initial coin offerings.' ICOs.

ICOs are a fundraising system that can be much quicker and efficient in the sourcing of much-needed funds than conventional venture capital establishments. However, ICOs also present some genuine risks. Time has unveiled countless ICOs to been fraudulent in their operations. The rate of ICO's that were labeled 'scams' in 2017 passed 80%.

The number of ICOs increased to 228 in 2017, from 46 that existed in 2016. This is according to data released by Coinschedule. The total value of funds raised through ICOs in 2017 was $3,6- billion. This value is over 37 times the total amount raised by ICOs in 2016.

The year also witnessed some uncertainty in Bitcoin with increasing debates on issues such as SegWit, which is a feature that was created to speed up transactions in the network. In addition to a "*slew of hard forks*," that placed some aspersions on the future of Bitcoin, and this led to volatility in the price and value.

Where we stand

By **February 2018**, the upgrade of Bitcoin with the Segregated Witness (SegWit) attained a scaling milestone. SegWit was first introduced into the Bitcoin ecosystem in August of 2017 to boost the speed of Bitcoin-related transactions. The idea was to move some of the transactions to an off-chain platform to reduce operational costs.

In **April 2018,** Bitcoin had attained a mining milestone of 17 million BTC. Blockchain.info released this figure, it means that there are just 4 million BTC that are waiting to be mined. The total expected number of BTC is 21 million which was projected to be mined by the year 2140.

In early **May 2018** the New York Stock Exchange revealed in a report that it would permit its customers to purchase Bitcoin. This report was also released in an article in the New York Times. The revelation was further enhanced by Goldman Sachs statement that by the second quarter of 2018 they would be open to Bitcoin futures.

Financially, Bitcoin and most other Blockchain-based projects had a rough **2018**. The values of large parts of the entire market have seen a strong decline, which is something that the space has experienced several times already. Countless inexperienced investors lost the majority of their capital to an up to 85% decline in value. It has been a progressive year, however, in the development of new applications and increasing transaction volumes.

In **February** of **2019**, JP Morgan Chase, the largest bank in the United States and sixth largest bank in the world announced the development of their own cryptocurrency. JPM Coin is a USD-backed currency for cross-border payments, security, and settlement,

The Blockchain community grows stronger and stronger by the day. More startups, investors, developers, and users get involved in one way or another in order to heighten it's relevance to today's economic and social world. Institutional spending on the technology is steadily increasing, and regulation is making way in numerous countries around the globe. The technological hypotheses of five to twenty years ago are steadily becoming a reality.

Companies and corporations around the globe are spending significant time and resources to develop new applications and patent their innovations, even in the face of high short-term development costs.

Countless prestigious and well-respected entities and major institutions have remedied their fearful stance towards the decentralizing technology, and the focus is shifting from learning and exploring the potential of Blockchain to identifying and building practical business applications.

What we can expect

With Blockchain, you have a decentralized system, one that is open-sourced, fair, and transparent. There are by, all means, plenty technological challenges that we have to overcome before we can build genuinely distributed, self-governing sovereignties, which include: The process of verification, data limits, and transaction speed.

We are, however, well on the way and with an exponentially accelerating improvement of the technology, not far off from viable mainstream applications.

A common issue with networks like Bitcoin is the energy consumption, while the ASIC race has seen PoW-governed networks become increasingly centralized, with a handful of mining pools dominating control. This limits the number of individuals participating in the technology due to the high costs. But these are mainly a challenge for the Proof-of-Work algorithm and not Blockchain itself, which can be modified, removed, or replaced.

As Blockchain technology improves, so too will the individual network. All issues that critics are currently concerned with can be remedied with technological modifications. Technological challenges of the hardware and software are clearly visible and under siege.

It must be mentioned that Blockchain faces a lot of resistance from governments that have traditionally generated and regulated currencies. With cryptocurrencies now making serious inroads into the mainstream, some governments fearing the devaluation of their FIAT, have been reluctant to adopt both cryptocurrencies and Blockchain technology. Yet, the potential of Blockchain is undeniable even to countries like China that banned Bitcoin, while simultaneously investing and advancing Blockchain technology. Not even these nations can deny the impact of the technology.

Governments, however, might decide to deliberately slow down the pace of adoption in order to lessen the resulting shocks and allow time for readjustment. Or, as Yuval Noah Harari detailed, *"Government regulation can successfully block new technologies even if they are commercially viable and financially lucrative."*
The technology can be delayed, stalled, and stifled by governments and institutions, yet the biggest obstacle to blockchain's more widespread use is cultural.

The very way that most people and organizations look at it and its potential to redefine their businesses is holding the technology back. Specifically, organizations should stop looking at Blockchain as a 'new' technology, because it's really not and individuals must learn to differentiate between technological obstacles and cultural misperception.

Finance is the context in which Blockchain is most commonly talked about. If people have heard of Blockchain at all, it will be in the context of Bitcoin, and the limited and always inaccurate and misrepresentative attention that it receives in the media, which is almost exclusively about Bitcoin and what it means for traditional finance, with other applications of Blockchain seen as niche or a long way off. In online communities, a overwhelming majority of the dialogue revolves around token value.

Problems that Blockchain addresses are not only the visible ones we are all aware of but societal issues that we all have accepted to be unchangeable and without solutions.

Paul Snow explained, "*Blockchains hold the promise of creating validate-able information and proving information did, in fact, come from intended sources.*"
It provides a viable solution to the increasing problem of fake news. Snow explained. "*The blockchain can confirm information to crack down on inaccurate or false reports and create responsibility for providing correct information. This would be a massive reform in politics, society, business, and government, and not through regulation - the reform is solely through math.*"

Blockchain provides answers to questions we have not thought to ask. Solutions to problems we did not know could we could fix. It is a disintermediation technology, a catalyst for societal and technological revolution and it's unsurprising that the response to such a bold proposal is to incite fear.

It's inevitable that we will create economic activity by transitioning to decentralized infrastructure. We are going to create jobs, we are going to create industry, and we are going to create a foundation for a sustainable civilization that the next generations can cherish and applaud. The technology is a vehicle we can use to truly deliver and establish economic justice in the world.

Nobody can know for sure what sort of impact Blockchain will have on different industries and professions in the future and it is extremely complicated to estimate the timetable of relevant developments, especially because they depend on political decision and cultural traditions as much as on purely technological breakthroughs.

"For the first time in 6,000 years of human history, we can have peer-to-peer exchange where trust is not a problem anymore. And it's through the technology that underlies bitcoin. It's called the blockchain."

Patrick M. Byrne

Part 3

An Evolutionary Step

We will explore several interesting heuristics in this section of the book. They are carefully selected and deliberately constructed and strive to encourage further exploration and inspire new and innovative ideas. To simplify the general idea and draw attention to specific notions, only the most essential aspects have been detailed.

We examine a new form of economic entity, only made possible through a distributed network running self-executing instructions. To make this book worthy of the 'maximalist' label, we combine these concepts with some of the recent breakthroughs in relevant technology to create two truly futuristic type of entities.

An autonomous delivery fleet of self-driving vehicles that transports all types of goods and an international education database for individuals in an ever more distributed landscape.

Followed by a systematic inspection of the potential impact on the different branches of government and ultimately pillars of society. We will extract an entirely new form of self-governance from our reasoning and dedicate some words to a new form of police for the people and by the people.

Blockchain levels the playing field in a world dominated by hierarchal thinking. A truly beautiful iteration of democratic governance has been made possible through it; we will look at how to get there and what to watch out for on the way.

We now stand at a point where we can literally design economic systems from the ground up. The fusion of Blockchain, Smart Contracts, and Consensus Mechanisms creates the possibility to build decentralized and autonomously governed network. Let's indulge some relevant quotes before we examine a distributed organization.

"If you recognize that self-driving cars are going to prevent car accidents, AI will be responsible for reducing one of the leading causes of death in the world."

Mark Zuckerberg

"Google is working on self-driving cars, and they seem to work. People are so bad at driving cars that computers don't have to be that good to be much better."

Marc Andreesen

"Self-driving cars are the natural extension of active safety and obviously something we should do."

Elon Musk

Decentralized Economics

The following words are dedicated to a new form of economic system. We will explore an autonomous and decentralized network, governed by Blockchain and coupled with AI. We will investigate how we can drastically improve the efficiency of conventional companies and services by eliminating many layers of the corporate and bureaucratic hierarchy. These networks will provide services at an efficiency that was not possible in the past.

We can see all major automobile manufacturers navigating to electric motors and autonomous driving. Let's take a look at some of the recent developments on that front.

GM acquired the self-driving startup, Cruise Automation, for $581 million in 2016. CEO Marry Barra stated, *"We expect to be the first high-volume auto manufacturer to build fully autonomous vehicles in a mass production assembly plant."* GM has not laid out any specifics or details regarding a timeline for their self-driving cars but announced the construction of a new research and development center for Cruise Automation through which 1100 jobs will be created.

GM acquired a 9% stake in the ride-sharing affiliate Lyft Inc. for $500 million as a plan to create a network of on-demand autonomous vehicles. GM plans the deployment of thousands of self-driving electric cars next year, in collaboration with Lyft.

Ford announced a $1 billion investment in Argo AI last February and plans to combine their technology with their own efforts to develop a fully autonomous vehicle. Ford will also initially utilize these vehicles for ride-hailing services. Mark Fields, CEO of Ford Motors, expressed the company's plan to have a fully autonomous vehicle in the market by 2021 and says that it will have, *"no gas pedal, no steering wheel, and the passenger will never need to take control of the steering wheel in predefined areas."*

Renault-Nissan CEO Carlos Ghosn states, *"So we know that autonomy is something of high interest for the consumers. This is the first brick — one-lane highway. Then you're going to have multi-lane highway, and then you're going to have urban driving. All of these steps are going to come before 2020. [...] 2020 for the autonomous car in urban conditions, probably 2025 for the driverless car."* Renault-Nissan is taking a different route than Ford and GM and partnered with Microsoft to advance their autonomous car efforts and plans to release ten different self-driving cars in 2020.

Volvo expressed their beliefs in self-driving cars in a $300 million joint venture with Uber to develop next-generation autonomous vehicles. Volvo bets that they will not only change the ride-sharing industry but the luxury car market as well. CEO Hakan Samuelsson states, "*It's our ambition to have a car that can drive fully autonomously on the highway by 2021.*"

Uber also partnered with Daimler to introduce their self-driving cars to Uber's ride share platform in the coming years. Daimler's efforts include a high-profile agreement with Bosch, one of their largest parts supplier and wants to bring fully autonomous vehicles to the market, "*by the beginning of the next decade.*"

BMW is working to get "*highly and fully automated driving into series production by 2021*" and has a notable collaboration with Intel and Mobileye to achieve their goal. Elmar Frickenstein, BMW's senior vice president for autonomous driving, states the possibility of fully autonomous cars by 2021.

To complete our global inspection of automotive manufacturers' plans for autonomous vehicles we need to include Honda's and Toyota's plans to have self-driving capabilities on highways by 2020.

No talk of autonomous vehicles is encompassing without the mention of American automotive manufacturer Tesla who has been equipping all their cars with all required hardware needed for full self-driving capabilities for years. Elon Musk, Tesla CEO, predicted that a Tesla will be able to drive from Los Angeles to New York City without human interference by the end of 2018.

The global automotive industry is undergoing major transformation on multiple fronts, the transition to electric and fully autonomous vehicles and a shift to ride-sharing services over personal ownership. The guys at Loopventures estimate it to fully take shape by 2040. These technologies are advancing at an accelerating pace, and the transition to fully autonomous vehicles will be one of the significant trend changes.

As previously established, some of the traditional manufacturers will capitalize on the emerging changes, but the competitive landscape of the industry will change dramatically with more and more tech companies bringing revolutionary technologies to the market.

Loopventures expect that by 2040, over 90% of all vehicles sold will be level 4 and 5, or 'highly' and 'fully' autonomous. The next decade will shape the transition to self-driving with an estimated 98,000 fully autonomous vehicles entering the market in 2020. The main hurdle for these advancements is legislative regulation, not techno-logical capability.

Truck driving remains one of the deadliest occupations in the United States, accounting for slightly more than a quarter of all work-related fatalities last year. According to the U.S. Department's Bureau of Labor Statistics, more than any other job in the country.

Large components of transport and logistics industries will undeniably be automated. There is absolutely no need for a human truck driver, subject to his inefficient day and night patterns, inaccurate senses, and unpredictable behavior if an autonomous truck, like the Tesla Semi, can provide a safer, more efficient, and more reliable service 24 hours, 7 days a week. Reducing accidents and death while dramatically increasing performance and profitability in this sector will drastically increase user trust and further stimulate the transition away from personal car ownership.

Combining our newfound knowledge of the current state of the autonomous vehicle industry with what we know about decentralized systems, we can conceptualize a very futuristic type of network and organization.

A delivery fleet populated entirely by fully autonomous vehicles, all communicating with each other and overseen by a variety of navigation and safety protocols. These protocols can be signed and deployed through a democratic process of consensus of the stakeholders.

The transport network automatically accepts new orders on the governing application, sends a part or a vehicle of the fleet to the desired location to pick up some form of transportable goods which is promptly and autonomously delivered to the desired location. This could be done through previously ordered containers or standardized packaging but does not require them.

A distributed infrastructure responsible for all management tasks removes the need for central governance like Uber and Lyft. In the words of Ethereum founder Vitalik Buterin, *"Whereas most technologies tend to automate workers on the periphery doing menial tasks, blockchains automate away the center. Instead of putting the taxi driver out of a job, blockchain puts Uber out of a job and lets the taxi drivers work with the customer directly."*

If we extend this concept with the coming changes in the automotive industry and the ability of machine self-governance thanks to Blockchain, we can elaborate how a consumer could transact directly with an autonomous vehicle or taxi without intermediaries. The network could consist of a single vehicle, or thousands.

A blockchain is deployed as a ledger storing all transactions and orders in an anonymous manner. However, providing all tokenholders with a transparent order book.

Don and Alex Tapscott, uncover that with Blockchain, the executives of public companies *"no longer need to swear that their books are in order once a year, their books will be in order every 10 minutes. Whether executive like it or not. No need for public auditors, the blockchain eliminates human error and prevents fraud in accounting. Shareholders and regulatory agencies alike will be able to examine the books at any point in time."*

The network will use an oracle to access the data provided by the autonomous vehicles. The third-party oracle we have studied previously comes to mind. We are working with a very real world application after all. The primary challenge with these is that people need to trust the sources of the information. Whether a website or a sensor, the source of information needs to be reliable and accurate. This is really a non-issue when the data collected by the autonomous vehicles is recorded and stored on the same chain. The accuracy of the data, however, is directly dependent on the accuracy of the sensors.

When drones start making their entrance in the global logistics industries, especially in the last miles of the delivery journey, we will see a number of projects utilizing this sort of infrastructure. A distributed database with its according Smart Contracts and Consensus Mechanisms accessing information provided by the nodes in the network corresponding to the machines in the real world. A native digital asset could serve as a means of ownership providing direct compensation for these nodes and the tokenholders. Productively monetizing machine labor.

Effectively these machines will employ themselves. The smart contracts are responsible for all transactions between nodes, not just between the users, but between users and machines, and machines and machines. With a limited range of governance, an autonomous vehicle can taxi passengers and fulfill deliveries and automatically receive and disperse the payment. Some of which can be stored for upcoming expenses like maintenance or energy. The excess will be distributed to the tokenholders proportionally to their stake.

Transparent networks transacting anonymous information and cryptographically secured databases will form the infrastructure for a new type of economic system. Distributed, digital networks that govern AI controlled machines in the real world, owned collectively by all stakeholders.

The benefits that these new systems carry over traditional ones, like greater speed and the possibility of entirely new business models far surpass the commonly referred to benefits like 'lower costs.'

As a matter of fact, the costs associated with transitioning from a centralized to a decentralized infrastructure are significant. Resources are rare, and the labor market is tight. 'Lower costs' usually refers to the transaction costs of individual transactions, not the cost related to developing and researching a new economic structure. However, even in the face of high short-term development costs, the shimmer of a thriving ecosystem has convinced many to take the step.

We are all aware of the fact that the advancement of autonomous vehicles and other automating technology corresponds directly to a decrease in reliance on human labor. Adding the streamlining and entangling of bureaucratic infrastructure through Blockchain into the mixture, we can't help but feel frightened. This technological synergy renders large sections of existing hierarchies, in addition to the actual labor itself, obsolete.

One does not need to contemplate these statements extensively before a foul taste starts forming in ones' mouth. The jobs of millions of people are at risk. It is potentially a very bitter fruit. However, not unavoidably so.

We cannot wait for these unprecedented technological and economic disruptions to break out in full force before we start looking for answers, by then it will be too late. We need to develop new social and economic models as soon as possible.

The philosophical challenges concerned with the emergence of an irrelevant or useless class and other global crisis, are outside of the scope of this book, if you are interested in them, however, I recommend *Homo Deus*, by Yuval Noah Harari. There are, however, practical challenges that society has to overcome when faced with an entirely new class of useless people that we will address.

Institutions need to shift their focus from their investors to their users and customers. Governments need to change and disband much of the representation for a more direct democratic approach. We need to accommodate the individual. Socially, economically, financially, and very likely, spiritually.

Blockchains' decentralizing nature, especially in finance, is set to stimulate economic entrepreneurship dramatically, enabling access to the global economy to all. This global push in economic prowess will have to be accompanied by a revolution in education and governance. In a rapidly changing world, education is a slow mover and largely depends on outdated and antiquated infrastructure.

"Nothing is more powerful than an idea whose time has come, and the time is right to marry education, AI, and blockchain."

Wilson Wang

Blockchain Education System

In our following examination of the impact of Blockchain on the educational sector of society, we will inspect, with the help of Donald Clark, how we can drastically improve existing aspects of the traditional systems. Concluding with an illustrious utopian vision of decentralized and indoctrination free education for the people.

The way in which the technologies will affect education can be examined on four levels. The lowest one being the single institution, which will use it to automate certification and accounting processes. The first problem addressed by Blockchain for institutions is that of unreliable certification. There are many causes for the issues relating to the validation, verification, and transportation when paper is used to prove one's credentials and certifications. It is a messy and antiquated system, waiting to be cleared up by a smart operator. The second obvious application for Blockchain is the streamlining of all internal accounting and management processes.

The San Fransisco software school, Holburton, offers project-based education as an alternative to college courses and has already used Blockchain to store and deliver certificates. To prevent false certification, encryption and two-factor authentication are used to create, sign-off, and secure the certificate in the network. Holburton does still provide students with hard copies, but a decentralized clearing number (DCN), created by the system, allows easy authentication by employers.

Although Blockchain's transparent and permanent nature means that records cannot easily be changed, the Hyperledger Fabric strives to increase students' privacy, as well. The Proof-of-Authority framework ensures that universities, wishing to view the records of a student, only have access to the latest information in authorized areas. At the same time, only accredited and identifiable nodes such as universities and institutions can edit Blockchain entries, which ensure that all information is reliable. All of this is done with a custom API that marries Hyperledger Fabric and Ethereum.

At present, MIT is experimenting with Blockchain, by enabling graduates to access their certificates via the Blockcerts app. This enables the university to accredit diplomas, while employees can be sure that all records can reliably be verified on the Blockchain. While Blockcerts was built on the Bitcoin Blockchain, it ultimately expanded to Ethereum and aims to work across any Blockchain network.

The second level refers to groups of educational institutions that cluster and cooperate, which exponentially increase the need for shared certification and achievement repositories. The group of universities, ANU, Boston, Delft, EPFL, and UBC, which recently concluded a certification and codeshare agreement, is one example.

Blockchain gives them a cheap, shared resource, regardless of the constellation of institutions or bodies.

Curiously, education is quite nationalistic. The third level contains nations. It's a devolved problem, even in the EU.

"A shared approach to the range of credentials produced at all levels of the system within a country, is essential: schools, colleges, universities, institutes, examination boards, trade associations, employers, etc."

There's a real need for an encompassing infrastructure that surrounds it all. Blockchain enables this solution.

The current certification system is really not suitable for its purpose in the modern world. The antiquated and inefficient, century-old infrastructure cannot accommodate the increasingly mobile and dispersed individuals of the 21st century.

In addition to ensuring authenticity, placing certificates on the Blockchain reduces the likelihood of loss, damage, and misplacement. A decentralized database of credentials and achievements of which only you have control, makes sense, especially when faced with an increasingly mobile population of students and employees.

Whether you move to another educational institution, a new job, a new country, and refugees, who do not have a copy of their degrees, there would be a form of secure, online repository.

The three levels we have examined so far are all extant; the infrastructure is there, the systems exist, even if they are outdated, these are aspects of traditional systems that Blockchain could advance. The next one, however, is exclusive to Blockchain and epitomizes its ability to transcend borders, oceans, and continents.

There are no international or global, certification databases. Employers must contact the universities directly without such a network, to validate any of the applicant's credentials. In turn, university admission offices must contact national registrars to verify the transcripts. This entirely redundant communication requires a lot of tedious back and forth.

We have the ability to place certificates and diplomas on the Blockchain on a global scale with the right technological infrastructure. Instead of having each of our universities and schools issue certified diplomas separately on their own Blockchains, they could all issue them within a single network. Although this is not in the interests of many educational institutions, it is an objective for some global players.

One such player is Sony, with it's Sony Global Education initiative, which already consolidates an online educational records depository on a Blockchain-based platform. Built on the IBM Blockchain and powered by Hyperledger Fabric 1.0, the system "*makes it possible to record and reference educational data and digital transcripts*" by accumulating data from "*multiple educational institutions.*"

Eventually, Sony aims to synchronize all kinds of data related to education, ranging from school registration, attendance, grades and lesson plans for students and educators. To create a single education profile for users. Students can also compile all their academic grades, and records for official use in a digital transcript. They want the service to be used by schools and universities and institutions and organizations so that people can share data with third-parties such as employers or LinkedIn.

A Blockchain network can offer a viable way to deal with official accreditation, making the problems of openness, scale, and cost of badges negligible. Massive open online courses truly transform the delivery of education and are a real catalyst for change. Despite the carping, people continue to make and take them.

The issue of certification, however, remains a little vague. Each MOOC provider issues their own certificates. With some imagination, secure accreditation in the form of agreement between major providers could boost the real demand for MOOCs. These open courses are about decentralization and widening access, so organizers have every reason to expand access to their certification.

It is challenging to deliver continued professional development (CPD), often fragmented, and poorly tracked. Imagine a Blockchain network that reliably tracked progress, training, education, and achievements within a profession, taking CPD data from attendance at conferences, courses, company training, and other forms of learning. Teachers and other professionals could receive input from trusted providers and be encouraged to do more CPD if these experiences and learning opportunities were credibly acknowledged in a reputable system.

Companies provide their employees with vast amounts of training, but storing performance is not easy. Current technologies for learning and talent management, SCORM, et al., are old and tired. A more open and secure system for use by employees is needed. Throughout a profession and independent of the individual institutions, not only internally.

Vocational education is now a big business, as governments around the world recognize the foolishness of relying too heavily on purely academic institutions to provide education after school. In the United Kingdom, a system of three million apprenticeships is financed by a payroll tax. It is a complex business, as employers play a stronger role in the management and delivery of training.

How will this process and certification be managed?

Blockchain is a viable solution, by providing a single, neatly distributed national and international infrastructure for both process and certification authentication.

Another way in which Blockchain affects education is by providing an efficient platform for micropayments. Traditional financial transactions use costly third-parties, while Blockchain allows almost free inter-party transactions.

This could open up the use of an educational resource-based fee structure. It opens up the possibility of pay-by-lecture, pay-by-video, pay-by-course, or even pay-by-page systems, and if most students agree that a lecture has not been delivered, no student is charged.

It liberates the system by making it more open and transparent.

National academic systems are clearly and completely corrupted by government money and politics, the curriculum is always determined through its accordance with the political agenda of the governments funding it.

In a free-market economic system, however, no self-respecting university would want to teach its students things that are obviously wrong and absurd as they strive to provide the most useful knowledge to them.

With a global perspective on education, we can distinguish between national narratives and fact, providing a platform for, while simultaneously rewarding those who provide qualitative, unbiased education. Rewarding indoctrination free education.

The education system will likely shift into a subject based service in which different, smaller institutions offer specialized services which are secured and certified on the Blockchain. You could travel and decide to take a course elsewhere or do so online which will still be secured in your encompassing profile. Everything counts and works. Hooked up to an international Blockchain to store and secure all information over which only you have control.

Institutions' main function is to lower uncertainty in the transaction and exchange of value. They provide a common source of trust between participants. Universities, for example, are trusted 'brands' in education. In finance, banks serve this function, creating an environment in which Blockchain's advantages are readily apparent.

"In education, however, there needs to be trust beyond the technology." We are looking at a hybrid model rather than a complete Blockchain takeover.

Blockchain clearly has individual, institutional, national, and international applications in the world of learning. It is relevant in all sorts of contexts: schools, colleges, universities, MOOCs, CPDs, companies, apprenticeships, and bases of knowledge.

Contrary to the outdated hierarchical structures, with a Blockchain-based infrastructure, the focus shifts onto the technology, with trust migrating towards it and away from the institutions.

Education is a slow learner and a very slow adopter. Despite its obvious advantages, the learning world is likely to be reluctant to implement this technology, as most of the financing and culture are focused on the individual institution. *"The stimulus for change will have to come from elsewhere."*

"Students have their eyes open and are looking for alternatives. Perhaps, like Bitcoin, the Blockchain revolution will ultimately come from left of field." Transformative change in education, however, is not possible without transformative change in governance.

"You can fool all the people some of the time, and some of the people all the time, but you cannot fool all the people all the time."

Abraham Lincoln

Blockchain and Governance

Large, slow to adapt, traditional, and non-intuitive institutions will be able to benefit the most from the coming developments and changes in technology. The apex of these slow bureaucracies, are our governments. Governments that can benefit dramatically in nearly all branches and aspects. Much of the existing hierarchies and processes can be eradicated entirely to gain much-needed transparency and unprecedented efficiency. Blockchain is the ax to the tree of hierarchy and bureaucracy. We will dissect several current branches of government in this section of the book.

Blockchain has already begun to infiltrate governments and corporations. Numerous countries and communities are working towards becoming the epicenter of Blockchain and decentralized technologies and have been pushing their advancement. Utilizing Blockchains to secure and record governmental election processes is not a new concept.

123 out of the 192 countries in the world can be considered at least partial democracies. This means that they depend on electoral consensus to appoint officials and decide on national referendums.

Conventional voting systems are some of modern governance's most outdated, inefficient, and manipulation-prone aspects. Blockchain can be implemented to efficiently and continuously trace the validity of every single ballot without infringing on the privacy of any single voter. The ledger also eliminates the risk of voting result manipulation in corrupt countries, by replacing the central point of processing with an effective Consensus Mechanism.

The crypto valley in Zug, Switzerland has recently successfully completed a Blockchain-based voting trial. "*The premiere was a success.*" Dieter Müller, the chief of communications in Zug, stated after the pilot.

Japan is also in the avant-garde of the technology with the city Tsukuba leading the country's first Blockchain-based digital vote. The system will use the Japanese social security card equivalent to verify the identity of the elector. According to the Japan Times, the solution is currently being used to allow citizens to vote on "*social contribution projects.*" The system will use Blockchain to prevent any recorded data from being altered and falsified.

West Virginia has completed Blockchain-based voting, this 2018 mid-term election season. Voatz, a mobile election provider facilitated the mid-term state election and worked with policymakers to carry out a mobile voting pilot for all active uniformed and overseas citizens. The mobile voting project was financed by a philanthropic arm of Tusk Holdings and implemented by the Secretary of State of West Virginia, in order to make voting more accessible and safer for the disenfranchised population of overseas voters. During the 45-day absentee voting period, active UOCAVA voters from 30 countries and the United States cast 144 ballots.

Elections are not the only way in which Blockchain is being utilized. Look no further than Zug 's sister city Chiasso to find the emergence of mainstream Blockchain use cases that introduce a new era of decentralized government. This community on the Swiss-Italian border recently allowed its residents to make tax payments using cryptocurrency.

Local authorities in the United States have also recognized Blockchain's potential in the provision of public services. A number of projects have been launched that are currently at various stages of implementation. The state of Delaware announced the Delaware Blockchain Initiative for the first time back in 2016. Illinois announced the Illinois Blockchain Initiative, in 2017, calling on a consortium of agencies to cooperate in the exploration of state-relevant, Blockchain-based innovations.

Wyoming has enacted several pro cryptocurrency and Blockchain laws over the past years, the most recent legislation, SF125 clearly recognizes property rights for digital assets.

The Blockchain-based Brooklyn Microgrid in New York was developed specifically for households who want to buy and sell solar-powered electricity, with the first transaction occurring in April of 2016.

Individual citizens are turning to Smart Contracts to solve their old and accepted problems. These initiatives provide an insight into how governments can implement the technologies in the future.

Estonia is another example of a country eagerly striving to become the Blockchain capital of the world. Distributed ledgers have been implemented in the countries judicial, legislative, security, commercial, and national health systems, since 2012.
The Estonian government has pushed the technology past the experimentation stage into mass adoption to provide its citizens access to and control over their personal data.

The Australian government has signed a five-year, $740 million US dollar deal with IBM to provide Blockchain, Automation, and Artificial Intelligence to Australian federal departments, including defense and home affairs and to improve data security. It is a significant step forward in Australia's aggressive strategy to be one of the top three digital governments by 2025.

While some countries like Estonia and Australia pursue many different aspects of Blockchain to improve and remedy issues plaguing their current models of governance, a select few are betting on the technology for an entirely decentralized government.

One of these is undoubtedly, Dubai, which is striving to fully transfer their infrastructure and replace the existing system to process complex government transactions on a Blockchain.

Dubai is considered one of the world's most digitally advanced cities. It has everything an avid futurist could desire, flying taxis, unmanned trains, automated sensors, and smart solar panels. The Emirates authorities, however, are not content with what they've already achieved and actively implement the most innovative ideas in their strategy to make the city the first smart megapolis based on Blockchain by 2020.

They are preparing to transfer their entire government infrastructure and economy onto a Blockchain to reduce clunky documentation in the movement of goods and information in the state. All circulation of documents will be carried out in electronic form, and bureaucratic processes like starting a business will be drastically simplified for citizens.

By 2020, the UAE city wants to digitally transact all bill payments, license renewals, and visa applications which account for more than 100 million documents each year. *"The local authorities plan to create a paperless digital space in the private and public sectors."*

Sultan Butti bin Mejren, the general director of DLD, stated: *"Our aim is to unite all real estate and department services on a single platform."* While the grand vision of H.H. Sheikh Mohammed bin Rashid Al Maktoum is to make "*Dubai the first city fully powered by Blockchain by 2020*" and thus make it the happiest city on earth. The strategy will be using three strategic pillars: Government Efficiency, Industry Creation, and International Leadership. This initiative is no longer in a stage of infancy.

Dubai ranks first in the world in the number of projects being implemented, including those in which Google, Uber, Amazon, IBM, and other corporate giants use Blockchain. Thanks to the Smart City program that launched in 2014, which involves the gradual implementation of more than 545 projects that will dramatically alter the interaction between Dubai and it's residents and visitors.

The smart city concepts integrate AI influenced Blockchain governance with the Internet of Things. They will use sensors and machines to automate and optimize the infrastructure for their residents. Smart cities fully automate urban processes and services, they optimize traffic, energy usage, and the circulation of information. Traffic lights that adapt their rhythm based on the current load. Solar panel road lights that efficiently adapt and brighten with movement in the proximity.

McKinsey analysts predict that the number of smart cities worldwide will reach 600 by 2020, and nearly 60 percent of the world's GDP will be produced in them five years later.

Another critical aspect of governance that Blockchain will revolutionize is notarization. Administrative timestamps validate the exact time at which an action takes place in a citizen's life, ranging from events such as birth and death, to when new identity documents are received, educational certificates are updated, or ownership titles are exchanged. Most of these processes are still carried out either in isolated databases or through brick-and-mortar bureaucracies, prone to errors. The encrypted nature of the data on a chain, also means that all of this information is safe and only visible to the owner or authorized parties, which could exclude the authorities themselves.

While only a select few countries are developing a fully decentralized government, many started by utilizing some aspects of the technology for economic gain. Fortunately, this is one of the ways through which the allure of Blockchain infiltrates governments and corporate institutions. The promise of secure data storage with reduced costs and efficient streamlining of bureaucratic processes will initiate a domino-like fall of larger and larger responsibilities into the autonomous hands of a borderless and global network.

Despite the challenges of nation-states in solving global problems, they are the primary form of geopolitical organization for the foreseeable future. Their function, however, will likely shift dramatically.

The encrypted, decentralized, and agile methods of storing information pioneered by a future government based on Blockchain will lead to a more responsive and user-friendly interaction between the individual and the authorities. The use of the decentralized ledger to process administrative procedures improves the security of documentation and processing power of governmental interaction, while at the same time enabling citizens to reduce time-consuming and frustrating bureaucracy and office lines.

Control and distribution of social welfare have proven to be slow and prone to corruption in many developing countries and emerging economies. Third-world authorities do not have the infrastructure to manage government payments effectively and rely on third-party systems.

As is the case with voting and documentation, it is straightforward and beneficial to implement a Blockchain as a trustless ledger in the transparent and reliable managing of social welfare funds. Countries that may not be lucky enough to provide reliable, traditional, and centralized infrastructure can use Blockchain to manage and distribute the funds efficiently.

We will touch on the sensitive subject of police next.

"If the machine of government is of such a nature that it requires you to be the agent of injustice to another, then, I say, break the law."

Henry David Thoreau

Protector of the People

To establish certain 'Anhaltspunkte' of knowledge, we will inspect the origin story of the police force, which technically stretches back several millennia. We must not, however, journey back in time to the ancient, great civilizations of Egypt, Persia, Rome, and China to paint an encompassing image, primarily because the origin stories are so strikingly similar.

Our examination is well-rounded with our discussion of the historical events in the middle ages leading up to the origins of modern police, which we will explore with the help of David Whitehouse. It is irrelevant for our sake to inspect the history of police farther back than that.

'Police,' stems from the Middle French *police*, in turn from *politia*, which is the latinization of the Greek word *politeia*, which stands for "*citizenship, administration, civil polity.*" In ancient Greece, "*politeia*" represented all authorities and the power of the head of state to ensure compliance with the law.

Before police was established as a 'prevention' measure for riots, strikes, and major demonstrations, towns and cities did not necessarily require an 'enforcer' agent, especially not one that gave tickets and exercised casual intimidation over the people.

Communes were self-governing towns and cities in the 11th and 12th centuries, in France. The communes did occasionally assemble small armed forces and militia, made up of townsmen and had their own courts, but neither of the two was responsible for bringing people up on charges. With a high degree of social equity, which provided a strong sense of mutual obligation, it was you, the citizen, who would press charges if you got robbed, assaulted, or were cheated in a business deal.

Over the years, however, class conflicts intensified. The nobles responded with increasing violence. Any civil unrest would be handled in one of two ways. The leaders hung, or the army ordered to forcefully disperse the crowd.

Several centuries passed, and the middle ages saw civil movements ended this way predominantly. However, more and more violence was required for the ruling class to suppress the population, but there was no police like force.

The industrial revolution in England combined with the growth of British cities produced new outbreaks of struggle and catalyzed by the French Revolution in 1789, resulted in radical change. The revolution overthrew the monarchy, established a republic, and culminated in a dictatorship under Napoleon, which catalyzed violent periods of political turmoil.

The British ruling class became fearful of the English people following the French lead and took stronger measures against public unrest. Meetings of over 50 people were outlawed.

Over the next three decades, however, the English gathered in bigger and bigger crowds to protest, riot, and strike. The nobles started to respond with their armies, which proved a most ineffective approach to crowd control. It provides mainly two possible outcomes. The army can refrain from shooting, letting the crowd proceed. Or actively kill citizens, producing working-class martyrs. Neither of the two produces a desirable outcome if your goal is to maintain your superior status.

This is precisely what transpired in 1819 when a crowd of 80,000 gathered to demand the reform of the parliamentary representation of the people. On the 16th of August, the cavalry was sent to the St. Peter's Field, in Manchester, England.

Misinterpreting panic from the masses as an attack, the regiment was ordered to disperse the crowd. The 15th Hussars charged with sabers drawn. Killing 15 and injuring between 4- and 700. The abominable action was later coined the Peterloo Massacre and provoked a wave of strikes and protests.

Even the proven and time-honored practice of publicly executing the movement's leaders lost its effectiveness. While executions exert an intimidating effect on small crowds, they simply enrage large ones of thousands of supporters.

The ruling class needed a new approach to crowd control and civil unrest, and it took just ten years following the Peterloo Massacre for the London police force to be founded in 1829. This new force was established to disperse crowds while avoiding to create martyrs and was equipped to inflict nonlethal violence.

Now, any force organized to routinely deliver violence will occasionally kill some people. *"But for every police murder, there are hundreds or thousands of acts of police violence that are nonlethal — calculated and calibrated to produce intimidation while avoiding an angry collective response."*

When the London police were not concentrated in crowd control squads, they were dispersed to the city to police the poor and working class's everyday life.

This summarizes the distinctive dual function of modern police: The dispersed form of surveillance and intimidation in the name of combating crime, and the concentrated form of activity against strikes, riots and major demonstrations. *"That's what they were invented for — to deal with crowds — but what we see most of the time is the presence of the cop on the beat."*

The evolution of the force in the States progressed simultaneously. The 1828 riot and a series of major riots over the following decade accelerated a series of incremental reforms that eventually led to the establishment of the New York City Police Department in 1845.

The reforms expanded, professionalized, and centralized the force with a more military command chain. It was expanded to 24 hours and taking a second job was forbidden to police officers. The pay was increased, and officers no longer received a portion of the fines.

The story in the south, as you might expect, is a little different. The Charleston police force's precursor was not a set of urban guards, but slave patrols operating in the countryside. As one historian put it, *"throughout all of the [Southern] states [before the Civil War], roving armed police patrols scoured the countryside day and night, intimidating, terrorizing, and brutalizing slaves into submission and meekness."*

The slave masters adapted the rural methods to city life over time. The Charleston population did not explode like it did in New York and there were still only about 25,000 people living there in 1820. More than half of them, however, were African Americans.

Since conditions were dramatically freer in the urban south than on the plantations, the state had to step in to carry out the repressive work that the slave masters usually took care of themselves.

By the 1820s, the Charleston guard and watch developed into a recognizably modern city-run police force, harassing the Black population at night, while staying on call for rapid mobilization to control uprising crowds.

Blacks, even free Blacks, caught without an acceptable excuse after curfew, were arrested overnight and subject to up to 39 lashes after a judge looked at the case in the morning. Even early on, the first significant difference was that the Guard was a paid force instead of a group of conscripted citizens.

The city guard also monitored and policed the weekly markets on holidays and Sundays, which were primarily operated by Black slave women. Meaning the people were harassed and intimidated.

The specific history of police forces varies from city to city and nation to nation, but they all tend to converge on similar institutional solutions. The nature of the police stems from the nature of the 'problem': An urban working population that has developed some economic autonomy as wage workers and craftsmen and has thus succeeded in creating its own self-assertive, collective life. The story in the south also reinforces what was already clear in the North: *"Anti-Black racism was built into American police work from the very first day."*

Corrupt and violent governments often modify their police force into weapons of systematic suppression and intimidation. The processes of 'Verreichlichung,' in Nazi Germany initiated disestablishment of the police, resulting in a re-shaping of the force into a suppression tool of the Führer, while simultaneously lifting the legislative chains that held this dog back until then. It closed its ties to the NSDAP-Organization Schutzstaffel. There are plenty of other relevant examples throughout history.

The police institution has never been a response to crime, and it really did not enforce any new ways of dealing with it. The most common method of resolving crime, before and since the creation of the force, has been for someone to tell them who did it. Besides, crime has to do with the acts of individuals, and the ruling class invented police in response to challenges posed by crowds.

Body cameras have been implemented in Ferguson, Missouri, and numerous other places in the United States like Las Vegas, Nevada and across the globe by the Swedish Stockholm Police, Hong Kong Police, the South Australian Police, and countless more.

These, however, have been largely ineffective. While they can improve behavior on a superficial level, once push comes to shove, deeper rooted biases come to light and instincts take over. As Dan Honig, an assistant professor of international development at Johns Hopkins SAIS and Jayme Johnson, an adjunct professor in the Department of Justice, who worked 10 years in London's Metropolitan

Police, said, *"If the instinct to use force is deeply ingrained, it doesn't matter whether a camera is rolling."*

Body cams have been an ineffective measure against police brutality, discrimination, and intimidation. But if this footage is automatically uploaded and permanently secured on the Blockchain and viewable by all nodes, then no racial injustice can occur without coming to the network's attention. The prying eyes of the public are ever-watching. Any registered node can initiate a voting process, removing a public servant from his duties, which places the agents directly into the palm of the people they are serving. These voting processes can be decided by majority vote and can automatically be enforced once they have concluded.

The law enforcing organizations in the majority of the world consist of outdated, inadequate, oppressive, corrupt, and slow infrastructure. For the first time in history, we are able to establish a force that truly and entirely corresponds and matches the definition of the police. Protector of the people, by the people.

The duties of these officers are transparently encoded into the public employment contracts.
They can publish proposals to the network and have a certain type of executive power decided upon by the token-

holders. For example, the agents are able to give tickets on their own, but the democratic vote will determine whether they would do so entirely.

There are close to 200 million surveillance cameras installed across the country of China, four times as many as there are in the United States. The Chinese authorities expect to integrate private and public cameras, by 2020, leveraging the country's technological expertise in facial recognition to build a nation-wide surveillance network. Chinas mass surveillance and social scoring, are manifestations of a technological nightmare that should remain in the Black Mirror episode it emerged from.

The marriage of Blockchain and AI birthed a beautiful solution to increase safety without sacrificing privacy. We can now create networks of cameras that use artificial intelligence and facial recognition in an effort to fight crime without giving up much of our privacy. The cameras can act independently and autonomously compare faces to an open and strictly enforced database of targets. All known persons of interest and criminals might be in this database. The key advantage is that all of the video is automatically stored and cryptographically secured from all on a Blockchain. A registered facial match with the database is required before the Smart Contracts unlock the video or grant access to authorized parties, like the police forces or criminal investigators, media outlets, or the public.

This is a means of improving the security and safety of the people through public surveillance without sacrificing our privacy.

I want to make a personal note here that I do not believe any degree of public surveillance is required or just, however, a hybrid model is possible.

We now possess the capabilities to create fair, centaur infrastructure consisting of humans and machines to service the public need for safety and security without infringing on their personal lives, rights, and privacy. These centaur policing organizations will require engineering teams that code, maintain, and oversee the analytical and technical components of the network and AI.

In a machine governed system, human emotions, desires, and fears are a non-factor. Greed, jealousy, anger, and irrationality are no longer interesting. Networks where the desires of the many are superior to the ones of the few.

Any sized municipal community, town, city, city-state, or country can collectively collaborate to create a network that employs humans and machines, like cameras. The laws to enforce are decided upon in the network directly, the hierarchal internal structure must be transparent, and the employment of the agents, a matter of network consensus. The body camera footage is viewable by all, which would quickly remove all unfit, crooked, or bigoted and racist individuals from such positions.

For the first time in history will the execution genuinely and entirely correspond and match the definition. This model of public serving organization is readily applicable in other sectors like the fireguard or EMTs. It would theoretically also be possible to be used in case one would like to organize and fund a municipal militia or even nationwide army to fight the existing systems. The far more appealing and desirable options, however, would be for the existing entities to migrate to the new model of governance. It is only in the interest of all citizens.

This said, there are other more effective measures available to decrease police brutality and racial biases. These range from increased training, in duration, intensity, length, and range, to other deescalating measures and regulations during the policing.

We needed to establish a common knowledge of the accepted, yet unreasonable and outdated fact that police still largely only serves the two main functions it was created for centuries ago. The intrusive surveillance and unnecessary intimidation in the name of fighting crime; and the concentrated function to take on strikes and riots.

There are several distinct 'Anhaltspunkte' that we have established previously that we will aim to merge in the following section. Encompassing, private profiles, decentralized economics, centaur organizations, with distributed finance.

"Good government is no substitute for self-government."

Mahatma Gandhi

Political Philosophy

Before we indulge in our vision of a decentralized government, economy, and ultimately society we should ask ourselves a more fundamental question. A more philosophical question if you will.

Do we need any form of government at all?

The anarchist view is that to be governed means, to be *"watched, inspected, spied upon, directed, law-driven, numbered, regulated, enrolled, indoctrinated, censored, commanded, by creatures who have neither the right nor the wisdom nor the virtue to do so. To be governed is to be at every operation, at every transaction noted, registered, counted, taxed, stamped, measured, numbered, assessed, licensed, authorized, admonished, prevented, forbidden, reformed, corrected, punished. It is, under pretext of public utility, and in the name of the general interest, to be placed under contribution, drilled, fleeced, exploited, monopolized, extorted from, squeezed, hoaxed, robbed; then, at the slightest resistance, the first word of complaint, to be repressed, fined, vilified, harassed, hunted down, abused, clubbed, disarmed, bound, choked, imprisoned, judged, condemned, shot, deported, sacrificed, sold, betrayed; and to crown it all, mocked, ridiculed, derided, outraged, dishonoured."*

If this description sounds too rhetorical or too politically prejudicial to you, *"turn to the Oxford English Dictionary for a definition of government: it says that to govern is to rule, conduct, regulate, command, curb, control, sway, influence and determine. These are the same as verbs which Proudhon uses, but they are in the active tense - the tense of the 'doer'. Most of us receive government in the tense of the 'done to'."*

Now, I enjoy linguistic acrobatics as much as the next man, which is why I included it, but scouring the nearest thesaurus to elaborate your argument does not usually solidify the lacking foundation of your theory.

A question to the average anarchist arises: Why are you so bitter?

Governance is not always the suppression and control of one people over another. Political philosophers have debated these issues for millennia and have justified one form over the other extensively in voluminous writing and extensive literature. We will examine some of the various proposed forms of governance, before clarifying our own perspective.

The Republic

The Republic, a Socratic dialogue, was published by Plato in 380 BC. It separates people into two classes, those with an economic function and those with a ruling function. The economic class may live in a capitalist structure, but the ruling class of guardians and philosophers lives in secluded communities and nuclear families without private property. Plato is trying to utilize this separation to prevent the ruling class from following the allure of private interest instead of the interest of the people. The guardians hold all political power and have no economic role.

The guardians would surely be thoroughly educated, and the economic class would not need to concern itself with political matters, but they are nevertheless governed by people who live entirely different and separate lives from their own.

Plato draws an analogy with the soul and separates the guardians, *reason*, and their assistants, *spirit*, from most people with an economic function, *appetite*. These three in composition create a balanced whole.

If the state and the soul are similarly composed of *reason, spirit,* and *appetite*, does it make sense to divide people to serve only one of these functions? Does it make sense to cease to be a harmonic balance of all three?

This may lead to a balanced state in theory, but how can it lead to a balanced individual?

The Leviathan

Thomas Hobbes, an English philosopher in the 17th century, elaborated in his monumental work, Leviathan, that societies need a government, no matter what. They keep people under control and civilization alive. To Hobbes, no government is ever at fault, because the absence of government, good or bad, is much worse.

The political philosophy is based on two hypotheses: The 'natural state of man,' is a state of war and that everyone wants to avoid death. In his work, he describes the lives of people without governments as, *"nasty, brutal, and short."*

When the people concluded that the only way to avoid death and provide themselves with a safe and comfortable way of life, was to recognize a perpetual, sovereign authority, they sacrificed some of their freedoms by establishing a superseding power, against which each of them was impotent, to maintain order and peace.

Hobbes refers to this backbone of government, as the Leviathan, which guarantees law, order, and preservation. Living within the Leviathan requires you to accept a sovereign power over you because you fear that you could not survive without it keeping order.

The Social Contract

The Social Contract was published in 1762, almost a century after Hobbes, in which Jean-Jacques Rousseau, a Genevan philosopher, argued that the natural state of man, without governments, is one of peace and harmony, not war and disorder.

The Enlightenment movement spread throughout Europe following the American and preceding the French revolution, which was heavily influenced by European philosophers, such as John Locke, Baron de Montesquieu, Voltaire, and Rousseau, who elaborated in his Social Contract, that people would be better of with as little government as possible.

Even if there is a need for it, there must exist a social contract between the government and its citizens. A government must not be oppressive or censorious, yet powerful enough to serve the people effectively and thus make them happy. The government must respect it's people, so that the people, in turn, respect the government.

The problem with the *Platonic* and *Hobbesian* philosophies is that the majority of people lose their autonomy in the interest of authority. Advocates of social contract theories, such as Rousseau, argue that the solution to the conflict between authority and autonomy is democracy. But what does that really entail?

Representative Democracy

In theory, everybody participates in the government within a democracy. By disturbing the law-makers and the law-abiders, it combines the advantages of authority with the freedom of autonomy.

Rousseau states that "*every person, while uniting himself with all, [...] obeys only himself and remains free as be-*

fore." This is, however, only viable in a direct democracy, meaning that every law adopted and every choice made is decided by all individuals in society.

The theory falls apart on the common misconception that direct democracy is not possible on a large scale. In reality, the technology to facilitate said infrastructure was simply not developed yet. Without the necessary, trustless systems, people resorted to the next best option of representative democracy.

It is the model most of us are familiar with and involves the democratic election of political officials from a limited sample of candidates. The people will vote for the candidate whose views most closely resemble their own, based on the promises and statements they have made.

Prevalent and modern representative democracies come in different forms, but most are neither genuinely representative nor actually democratic. There are numerous apparent issues with this form of representation.

One cannot know which issues the officials will have to face in their term and can therefore not be sure that their views will be represented. Humans are unstable, and one can never be sure if they will change their political stance in concern to any regard.

And, one can never know for sure if the candidate is, in fact, striving to achieve what they claim or if they are pursuing private interests under a false facade. It is also impossible to have representatives for all views, as the complexities of representing the individual values are precisely why representative democracies substituted direct ones.

Thus, the people need to pick the candidates whose views most closely resemble their own, swallowing the aspects they don't agree with in favor of similar core values. Stripping away individuality left and right to fit citizens into predetermined political cookie cutters.

Current Model - USA

Citizens in the United States vote for the mid-term and presidential elections every four years. They are historically only ever presented with two different political platforms, which is obviously an incredibly skimmed scenario as no issue is ever distinctly black or white. A or B. 1 or 0. The opinions of individuals always spread neatly across a spectrum and being presented with two options is incredibly unnatural. People in the US often vote not for what they think is the right kind of government, but by what seems to be the worst option. They tend to conclude which choice is the worst for them personally and which is the worst for their nation and then choose the other, provided it has a chance of winning. There is a long history of people not voting for the middle party because they don't think it can win.

The U.S. Constitution contains the Electoral College process, which is one of the most unfit systems for proper representation and makes absolutely no sense in the 21st. century. We must not forget the facts. In the popular vote, Clinton received 2.87 million more votes nationwide than Trump. Trump is the product of an outdated, faulty, and utterly obsolete electoral and political system.

However, because the process is part of the U.S. Constitution, it is necessary to pass a constitutional amendment to change this system. The last of which was passed in 1992 due to a nearly unattainable two-thirds majority vote in the bipartisan system. Specific legislative changes need to be made for which the current system is vastly unprepared. It is inflexible and slow.

The situation is further complicated by the limited information the parties tend to market. Carefully crafted narratives are often promoted with the help of public relations and marketing agencies.

Politics is a big business, and the decisions of the people are influenced by those in control of the distribution of information through media. Living in a democracy like in the US is buying into the illusion that we participate in the decision-making, while in reality, a small hierarchal group of capitalists and politicians is in control.

Current Model - Great Britain

The model of democracy in Great Britain, and most western countries in fact, only bear minor differences between each other. In Great Britain, the citizens vote in a general election every four or five years. They usually vote for one of three main political platforms, with three slightly different economic variations

As it is in other representative democracies, people vote for the lesser of two evils and usually refrain from the moderate, middle party due to a low likelihood of winning. Politics in Britain is a marketing and advertising feast as it is in the states.

Self-Governance

Plato's Republic, Hobbes' Leviathan, Rousseau's Social Contract, and the representative democracies of today differ on many levels. There is, however, something that all of these and the overwhelming majority of political philosophies' have in common. All of these philosophies and the different models they detail rely on the starting assumption that self-governance is not possible, not at a scale of any meaningful size, and especially not at the scale of our civilization in the 21st century.

The reasoning is that, because a direct democratic system is infeasible, we must resort to the next best option. This is, however, no longer the case. We have the tools, we have the means, and we have the technology to facilitate a national and global infrastructure for self-governance. The philosophical aspect of self-governance and why we should care and migrate will follow next.

The growth of a population corresponds to the proliferation of differing opinions. From one end of the political spectrum to the other, governments are struggling to mitigate all sides.

The only way in which we can appeal to the desires of all sides, is by taking away the sides — removing the representatives.

Self-Governance eliminates bureaucracy; it is the only political philosophy in existence that cannot be used as a bureaucratic instrument imposed on one people, by another.

The Electoral College in the United States is a prime example of an entirely redundant aspect of modern governance that can entirely be replaced by trustless technology, while the only reason it will remain is the government's inflexible nature to change. If the mechanisms to amend and modify the system are too difficult, you're quickly stuck with an outdated model for hundreds of years.

Blockchain-based Self-Governance is inherently flexible as modification to the infrastructure can occur at the creation of any new block. All that's required is consensus.

This transforms government in society from a solid, inanimate object into an adaptable super-organism that, at any given time, is a true and accurate reflection of the people within it. Instead of an anomalous jumble of past and present, it would be a harmonic balance of ever-changing adjustments. The organic life would evolve with the contribution of all its members.

This political philosophy is by far the one that resembles natural life the closest. It is a philosophy that combines autonomy and solidarity. It believes in people instead of institutions, and the transition is inevitable.

History has taught us that there is usually a transitional period when one form of government falls and is replaced by another and this transitional process, is rarely peaceful. Take the fall of Rome, for example: After the collapse of the Roman Empire and the absence of Roman authority, Europe was left in a period of sieges, wars, invasions and all sorts of clashes from all around the world. This was a bloody period in which little was achieved in the way of achievement or prosperity and was adequately named the 'Dark Ages.'

The people of that time were so desperate for leadership and governance that primitive forms of government emerged in different regions in what was known as 'feudalism.'

Also, look at Poland's government at the end of the 18th century, South America at the middle of the 19th century, and various African and Asian countries after independence.

Hobbes is right to say that we need a strong form of government, but a government also needs room for people to express themselves constructively and creatively.

It is in all of our interest to work for a peaceful transition. Fortunately, this transition must not depend on the actions of the inflexible institutions, but the actions of the individual citizens. Once critical adoption of a network has been reached it becomes the local authority over traditional systems.

Anarchism

Anarchism is an attempt at self-governance, hidden behind revolutionary and populist terminology without any mention of the required infrastructure. We will dismiss it quickly as it's utopian ideals refer to nothing but self-governance without the infrastructure.

Decentralized Society

While contemplating ways in which Blockchain can improve or replace existing aspects of government is interesting, examining what is possible in an entirely new form of economy and society is far more appealing.

I understand that there's no point dreaming of an unattainable future. We may dream about our own Utopia, but we have to be realistic. We need to keep our feet firmly grounded in reality.

There are four pillars of a truly decentralized society that increasingly rely on each other for success and even survival. To live civilized and free, we need to have secure and unsupervised communication, clear and fair economic governance, transparent and efficient government, and a viable and decentralized currency. Let's examine these four pillars in detail.

Decentralized Communication

The foundation of any exchange or transaction, and in fact, interaction between humans is a means of communication. In a decentralized society, this communication needs to be private and uncompromised. It cannot travel via any centralized third-party, which requires the conquest of two technological challenges.

Firstly, it requires either a truly decentralized internet, as it was originally conceived, without ISPs and centralized data hoarding or a separate, peer-to-peer network. Secondly, secure and unsupervised means of communication in the form of an application built on said infrastructure. With these technologies in place, people can communicate with anyone they want, however they want.

The good news is that these challenges have largely been overcome. Efficiencies need to be gained, but applications for decentralized communication already exist, while problems associated with centralized communication are simultaneously becoming more widespread.

Centralized platforms, Facebook in particular, continuously lose more and more of their allure as people realize to which degree their data is harvested and sold. But even though people are growing suspicious of these social media behemoths, no significant migration away from the platforms has been noticed. Without a viable alternative, most people have watched the recent data scandals with resigned indifference.

Encrypted communications such as Telegram and Whats-App are a noble attempt at restoring users' privacy, but the information is still traveling through various central servers. There are also persistent rumors that these services are jeopardized by state actors and higher authorities.

There are nevertheless, numerous projects that have made notable progress on this front. Dedicated peer-to-peer messaging solutions like Tox Messaging, decentralized internets like Substratum, and distributed browser applications like Blockstack have all attributed to the advancement of private, personal communication.

All in all, communication is one pillar in which we have made significant progress, even if the problem of mass adoption is still huge.

Decentralized Law

I believe we have established and explored our philosophical stance on government and self-governance extensively enough. We will leave this subject behind and focus on a different, more technical aspect of it, the law.

Once we can communicate freely with each other, we need to be able to reach agreements, for which we need to be able to rely on common standards that we can choose to form contracts or define new ones ourselves. We then need to be able to be sure that these contracts are enforced.

The relevant literature in the Blockchain community has crowned Smart Contracts the victor of this battle. Various protocols support smart contracts which automate the execution of these agreements.

It is undoubtedly an impressive achievement to streamline the contracting process, but what happens when things go wrong? The dispute process is a larger beast to slay, even in traditional systems. If the contract is broken, in theory, there must be a condition within the Smart Contract that is met, to automatically revoke, terminate, or revert the contract. But what if the different parties disagree on the state of a transaction or about whether or not a contract was broken. Perhaps the conditions were missing in the first place.

The flippant answer is 'Write better contracts!'

But flawlessly encoding an agreement within a Smart Contract is beyond the skills of most non-technical people and, judging by the proliferation of bugged Smart Contracts, most developers as well. If most people are unfit to use a system, the system is at fault, not the users. Most current smart contract platforms are beneficial for large companies, which have many business processes that can be automated and streamlined in this way but are much less intuitive for ordinary people.

Individuals have complicated and sometimes perplexing needs and are prone to make mistakes and change their minds. The most viable scenarios seem to provide a variety of options, including, a choice of enforcer, a choice of adjudicator, and even a choice between different mediators and multiple legal systems. This is the original way in which our legal systems operated before centralism was invented.

Steve Omohundro, president of the Self-Aware Systems think-tank, said, "*Once the principles of how you codify law digitally become more understood, then I think every country will start doing it... Each jurisdiction would encode its laws, precisely and digitally, and there would be translation programs between them... Getting rid of the friction of all legal stuff is going to be a huge economic gain.*"

By experimenting with various approaches in different communities, projects like Libertaria can explore which ones work without jeopardizing the whole infrastructure.

Of the four pillars, Law is the most difficult to decentralize, so it's unsurprising that limited progress has been made, all of which has been slow and hard fought. We have inspected several projects that strive to improve aspects of governance with Blockchain, but they are mainly doing so in the form of improvements to existing centralized systems, such as increasing the transparency and efficiency of elections.

There is a dispiriting tendency to hand-wave legislative issues in decentralized projects, asserting that thousands of years of human development in this field can be encapsulated through proper use of Smart Contracts. But the real problem here is dispute management and not the contracts themselves.

Integrating human emotions, actions, and irrationality into any machine-governed, autonomous process tends to complicate things considerably. With century-old bureaucracies blocking any radical change, it is the pillar we've made the least progress so far, but there are plenty of projects pioneering the space and pushing boundaries on the daily, while legislation is giving way all around the globe.

Decentralized Economy

We have all chosen the private sector and corporations as the dominant institutions for the creation of wealth around the world. People sometimes argue that the opposite of the existing institutions is a fully planned economy, anarchy, or some kind of free agent nation that have proven to be unworkable, which could not be further from the truth.

The decentralization of economic systems and entities has little to do with the models of governance currently available in the world. On a global level, a decentralized economy refers to an entirely inclusive system to anyone in possession of a personal smart device. On the level of the individual entities and companies themselves, it relates to the bottom-up distributed stakeholder approach.

A decentralized economy would provide means of access to capital, funds, credit, partners, and customers internationally to individuals currently blocked out of the global economy in countries like Haiti and Thailand. It provides this access, regardless of the national legislative hurdles enforced by aid agencies in these nations.

The individuals will also have equal access to the distributed entities within the economy, which will be far more transparent. A Haitian artisan could buy a fractional stake of a company, as efficiently as a silicon valley hedge fund and would receive dividends or compensation just as seamlessly on his device. Some 1.7 billion people still don't have bank accounts. Financial inclusion is simplified without the need for financial institutions. The only thing required, for these 1.7 billion people, to join the global economy is an internet enabled device.

It also enables these individuals to design and create companies and economic structures with nothing but their device using building blocks in an application on their phone. Integrating only those bureaucratic processes they require and without governmental permission. It empowers the individual to an unprecedented degree.

The lack of financial tools essential to starting a business and the prevalence of government red tape make starting a business in many regions of the world challenging. Blockchain can supercharge entrepreneurship and therefore prosperity in many vital ways. The average person with an internet enabled device, living in the developing world, now has a reliable store of value and a way to conduct business beyond his community.

Although privacy and processing issues receive the majority of attention in decentralization circles, centralized production within the economy might be the biggest challenge we face. The technological capability to easily create and efficiently manage global supply chain logistics has transformed all aspects of all our lives.

This change may seem positive for many of us in wealthy countries: In recent decades, globalization has provided us with easy access to inexpensive food, products, and services that were unimaginable just a few decades ago.

And once again, the current decentralization tools are likely to aggravate the problem, not remedy it. Smart Contracts help global companies automate complex logistics processes and become even more ruthlessly efficient. True, the market is in theory open for smaller operations to connect and transact, but in practice, only existing behemoths will have the resources to pay gas prices to force their contracts through the network.

There are, however, some illuminating rays of light that shine on this bleak landscape.

There are, for example, several projects in various stages of implementation that strive to enable energy to be shared locally within your community without inefficient interaction with national grid systems. The Brooklyn Microgrid in New York is an example we've examined previously. Transparent and distributed economic entities will entail fairer and more sustainable resource cycles and supply chains.

Additionally, projects to tokenize natural resources on Blockchains aim to provide people with access to new sources of income, while simultaneously encouraging them to live more sustainably.

It is clear that the individual, not only in the developing world but especially in modern cultures, will benefit economically from the emergence of a decentralized economy with distributed entities, as the status of the most prevalent institutions for the creation of wealth shifts from corporations and companies to individual people.

It is difficult to determine whether changes in legislation will follow economic revolution or the other way around, there are plenty of historical examples for both scenarios.

The decentralization on both the level of the individual entity as well as the global economy is already underway. Governments all over the globe adopt increasingly friendly and progressive stances towards digital assets and their free trade and the regulatory landscape surrounding coins and tokens of different kind - i.e., security, utility - is becoming clearer as the fog of the unknown is being pushed away by strong winds.

"It is well enough that people of the nation do not understand our banking and monetary system, for if they did, I believe there would be a revolution before tomorrow morning."

Henry Ford

Decentralized Finance

A decentralized financial system is arguably the quintessence of a decentralized civilization. Only when the individual is in complete control of their economic power, can he use it in a free way, which requires a currency that is not minted by a central entity, that cannot be ceased by a financial institution. Private communication must include private transaction.

We need to be able to trade freely without intermediaries, including banks, if we so choose. Many people have devoted a lot of their time and energy to decentralizing finance, and with good reason.

We have not mentioned Bitcoin much as many others already have detailed the surrounding landscape extensively. We will touch upon it briefly now.

Money is an accounting system that facilitates wealth exchange. Money is not wealth. It is a means of credibly conveying information about value given, but not yet received, and for most currencies of today, this 'value' is little more than 'belief.'

What money really is, is a ledger. Fiat currencies like the US dollar, have a centralized ledger, managed by the US Federal Reserve, a private company. And this gives the central authority responsible for maintaining that ledger tremendous power, power that history has proven will inevitably be abused.

The Bitcoin Blockchain is decentralized, and that means that no one individual or entity has the power to arbitrarily create new units, seize or freeze your account, or block a particular payment from being processed.

"There are almost 200 currencies of the world, but there's only one international currency. There are almost 200 currencies controlled by central banks and governments, but there is only one mathematical currency today, and that is bitcoin. We are going to build more of them. Cryptographic currencies are going to be a mainstay of our financial future. They are going to be a part of the future of this planet because they have been invented. It's as simple as that. You cannot un-invent this technology. You cannot turn this omelette back into eggs."

Andreas M. Antonopoulos, one of the most profound and vocal voices in the space, detailed in his work, 'The Internet of Money.'

Bitcoin has monumental potential in several areas of society. To learn about these and the importance and relevance of sound money and the different monetary and economic policies plaguing modern society, please refer to the profound work, *The Bitcoin Standard,* by Saifedean Ammous in which he details that, *"Bitcoin offers the modern individual the chance to opt out of the totalitarian, managerial, Keynesian, and socialist states. It is a simple technological fix to the modern pestilence of surviving by exploiting the productive individuals that happen to live on its soil."*

He argues that, *"If bitcoin continues to grow to capture a larger share of the global wealth, it may force governments to become more and more a form of voluntary organization which can only acquire its taxes voluntarily by offering its subjects services they would be willing to pay for."*

From an individual perspective, however, separating yourself from established financial systems is still incredibly difficult. Cryptocurrencies are predominantly purchased on centralized platforms that require personal information for transactions of any significant size, which means you have a public entry point and if this entry point is known, the transparency of a Blockchain may actually make your transactions more visible than conventional systems.

The pseudonymous nature of all transactions in the Bitcoin network coupled with the public key cryptographic system means that if you know who is behind a given public address, you know all transactions that have ever gone to and came from that address, in addition to all addresses the target has interacted with, and their contacts and so on. It is easier to track Bitcoins in this manner than it is to track cash. There are other digital currencies like Monero who are addressing this issue to achieve an entirely anonymous currency.

If you're not lucky enough to be paid in cryptocurrency, it's almost impossible to purchase them in private. Platforms such as LocalBitcoins try to address this, but the applications often do not scale efficiently and are banned in many countries. This makes it paradoxically more difficult for digital currencies to escape their inaccurate associations with illegal and immoral activity.

Bitcoin offers us the monetary infrastructure for a world built purely on voluntarily cooperation. It provides us with the tools to be free from government control and inflation. *"It seeks to impose itself on nobody and if it grows and succeeds, it will be for its own merits as a peaceful and neutral technology for money and settlement, not through it being forced on others."*

This is the right moment to encourage you to experiment with Bitcoin, if you have not already, if only, as Andreas said, *"To experience the future of money. To gain a glimpse into an exciting technology. To learn about how money could be in the future and also become aware of how limited money and banks are today."*

Eutopia

It is clear that all four pillars of a decentralized society must be considered together to ensure that these technologies are not co-opted by the very centralized entities that they are designed to disrupt.

From small off-the-grid families to municipal communities, to millions strong metropolises. Individuals who want to should be able to combine these disruptive, foundational technologies themselves to live a fully decentralized life according to common philosophical, economical, and technological standards.

These communities can live together, free from any central authorities and control. As long as universal values and principles are established on a global basis, the different communities can follow their own charter and adopt any political or economic approach to self-governance.

The values most essential to life are established through an international infrastructure and will get increasingly granular the more local the network. Our general utopian vision details a decentralized society based on federated, self-governing communities following shared principles and core values.

Decentralization comes with the additional problem that we often hope to improve or replace the systems and actors that benefit most from new technologies. The very fact that they are established provides them with the resources and broad acceptance needed to adapt the latest technology to their own ends.

Digital technology could be the engine of economic progress, and Blockchain will be one of them without a doubt. It's not just about cryptocurrencies or payment services, but entire cities with all processes controlled by Blockchain.

A global, borderless civilization is at our doorstep. It is inevitable that the human race progresses into this new form of self-governance. As a civilization, we are facing major global challenges in the 21st century, from technological disruption to genetic engineering and global warming. The current systems are not fit to take on these challenges. All current centralized systems will slowly upgrade or be replaced by the alternative, and nearly all levels of the existing hierarchies will be rendered utterly obsolete. There is no way in avoiding the economic interest of the many.

Nationwide networks will be a natural stepping stone to a unified civilization. A couple major networks will most likely emerge that service most of societies needs and regulation. With several hundred thousand and millions of digital assets and decentralized networks consisting of only a handful of nodes.

An inclusive and at the same time empowering, borderless and free world community that can transact freely, entirely independent of geographical location and national regulation. Interconnected smart cities that track resources throughout the entire product cycle, advanced surveillance without compromised security. Seamless and unsupervised transactions between individuals throughout distributed economic infrastructure. Reliably and credibly tracked information and resources.

As Saifedean Ammous expressed flawlessly, *"For those of us alive today, raised on the propaganda of the omnipotent governments of the 20th century, it is often hard to imagine a world in which individual freedom and responsibility supersede government authority, yet such was the state of the world during the periods of greatest human progress and freedom.*

When government was restraint to the scope of protection of national borders, private property, and individual freedoms while leaving to individuals a very large magnitude of freedom to make their own choices and reap the benefits or bear the costs."

For the first time in history, individuals have a clear technical solution to escaping the oppressive and restrictive chains of the governments they live under.

Blockchain technology is already revolutionizing the machinery of government and how we can make it high performance, better, and cheaper. It's also creating new opportunities to change democracy itself. How governments can be more open and free from lobbyist control and elected representatives held accountable for the promises that got them elected. It has, for the first time in history provided a viable decentralized currency and served as the foundation for free and unsupervised communication.

Designing utopian systems in a vacuum ignores the fact that conceiving a new and better model is often the easy part: the problem is how to transition in a smooth and stable manner from the current system.

By itself, decentralized systems are quite simple and governed by fundamental economic phenomena. The complexities come in the messy intermediate stages, where the advanced technology coexists with traditional ones. The established systems won't disappear overnight, and the early transition phases are often the most hazardous and problematic.

Don and Alex Tapscott state that, "*according to Paul David, the economist who coined the term, 'Productivity Paradox', laying new technologies over existing infrastructure is not unusual during historical transitions from one technological paradigm to the next. For example manufacturers needed 40 years to embrace commercial electrification over steam power and often the two worked side by side before manufactures switched over for good. During that period of retrofitting, productivity actually decreased.*"

The emerging model of governance, however, is capable of accommodating continuous change. A Blockchain governed system can modify, edit, and alter all protocols and manuals at the creation of every block. There already are working prototypes of much of the technology needed to make this decentralization dream a reality.

Don and Alex Tapscott detail that, "The future is not something to be predicting, the future is something to be achieved. Like the first era of the internet, this blockchain era should not be governed by nation states, state-based institutions or cooperations. Yes, there is a role for regulation, however, blockchain must be primarily self-governed through the bottom up multi-stakeholder approach."

Many countries in the world have already embarked on the path to a digital economy, and we could very soon see qualitative changes in social, economic, and environmental aspects of life, without piles of papers, huge traffic jams, documentation errors, and double transactions.
However, it will take years for Blockchain to be integrated to manage urban services and public infrastructure, which will interact with IoT, Artificial Intelligence and Big Data.

The Blockchain revolution changes the way in which the individual positions themselves in the creation of wealth and public value in society and the establishment of order and law in governance.

Intense

The current state of the world is by no means close to any utopian ideal. All present models of governance are deeply flawed and the majority obviously corrupt. The coming generations are presented with a dying earth, and climate change seems to be a non-issue for the passing generations as global carbon dioxide emissions surged to record levels the year following the signing of the 2016 Paris climate agreement. The carbon footprint is too deep to ever wash away.

The global debt counter hit 185 trillion and greed remains one of the major driving forces in the economy. Millions of us across the world are unable to make a living outside of the system because we barely make enough to live while we work within it and yet almost every product we buy has someone living on just a few dollars a day hidden somewhere at the start of its supply chain. The system is out of control.

We fight overseas wars in the name of peace, yet the killing never ceases. The human race has yet to see a moment of global peace while millennia-old hatred and hostility are upheld by outdated dogma and indoctrination. We need to clarify and remove the doctrines of supremacy; the 21st century needs to be a time of peace, not war.

In a world where corporations run governments, and the rest of society follows in a muffling hierarchal structure, the individual has been left behind.

This is not a world you would want to live in as a member of the coming generations.

Blockchain, as a movement, as a shift in societal opinion, perspective, and reason, will impact the world at a grandiose scale. Blockchains allow anyone with a device to live and participate in the global economy and enable economic success for the individual in a borderless civilization. It is not just a scientific innovation, but a societal revolution.

There are good reasons as to why shifting to a global governance model and decentralized economic systems is a benefit, there are, however, real pragmatic challenges that I truly appreciate, but I don't think that they are sufficient excuses for an antiquated and ineffective model to remain in place, when the data is so clearly unfavorable.

Indulge my words, but do not extend my point too far. The title of this book was predetermined, and I deliberately attempt to advance the "Maximalist" perspective. I don't believe that Blockchain is a magic tool for world peace and equality. I am, however, saying that it is an effective catalyst for complete societal revolution and that a borderless civilization does have the means to achieve these goals.

The age of decentralization is another one of those extraordinary jumps forward in the evolution of our civilization.

I don't want you to get the impression that Blockchain is the solution to everything. The realities are that even though the technologies are evolving rapidly, many components are still in embryonic stages of development and the practicalities of decentralized living are still vague and hidden behind legislative obstacles.

Blockchain has such a monumental effect on the foundation of our economic systems that change will be slow and hard fought.

There is an interesting phenomenon that occurs several months into the discovery and personal journey of Blockchain. It is a phenomenon witnessed by many. All seasoned Blockchain enthusiasts will know someone who experienced it, if not themselves.

It has come up several times in dialogue with minds all over the world, and I have stumbled over it on message boards and forums, repeatedly.

It occurs after studying the subject to a certain degree of comprehension when suddenly the potential impact of the technology is realized. This manifestation becomes almost palpable. It is something truly beautiful, the understanding and realization that the world we live in does not need to be the way that it is and that we have the power to fundamentally change it for the better. The technology is so nuanced and transforms such a rudimentary layer of society. It is nothing short of mesmerizing.

As a matter of fact, I have not witnessed anyone who had a firm grasp of the concepts to doubt the potential impact. The realization is contagious, and there is no telling how many people can be captivated. It is so decisive that it almost reliably produces a similar behavior in different individuals.

Most critics and arguments against the technology are rooted in a lack of understanding. Skeptical listeners, especially those supporting traditional institutions, should first evaluate the proven benefits of Blockchain before dismissing it outright.

The Blockchain world is developing rapidly and what is sound and reasonable to think today might be wrong and outdated tomorrow. I attempted to maintain our feet deeply grounded in reality, while letting our imagination roam free.

Without doubt you have interesting and relevant information for the context of this book, suitable to be incorporated in volume two perhaps, but as Christopher Hitchens said, *"That's the great thing about writing a book by the way; You come into contact with all the people and arguments you should've met before you wrote it. But that's a common experience of authorship."*

I am looking forward to our coming discussions. Perhaps we will exchange thoughts over some hot black brew in small mugs or cool blond liquid in large glasses. Blockchain is a journey for me as it is for you and I would love for our paths to cross.

I will end this book by dedicating a few words to the people, the technology, and the nature of our world. We have long lost the close touch to nature that our ancestors once had, and we have been rapidly distancing ourselves from deep and honest human interaction. Most interactions pass through some technological medium, and we are continuously advancing that narrative. In a world with increasing technological surveillance and elaborate and detailed digital fingerprints, Blockchain enables us to regain power over our privacy and thus, our lives. We are currently seeing a movement, and a change in society take place that doesn't parallel the advent of the internet in its grandiosity and ambition, but the industrial revolution.

Our world is fit for fundamental change. We cannot watch the previous generations desperately clasp and hold onto old, outdated forms of governance and commerce. We cannot sit idle. This is our earth, our life, and our future.

Blockchain is the catalyst for societal and technological revolution. It is only one of the major disruptors of the 21st century, it will, however, drastically increase the potential of IoT and AI. They are paradigm shifters already, merge these together and you open a technological Pandora box. Ever-increasing waves of disruption that will shake and restructure society from the ground up. There won't be a single distinct event after which the civilization will simply settle into a new equilibrium; rather there will be a cascade of ever bigger disruptions. The mining of the Bitcoin Genesis Block 0 was the first.

Doing your part in this is straightforward. Adopt. Adopt the technology and the new ways of life. Build applications suitable for a new type of civilization and most of all vote and elect officials associated with this internal Blockchain revolution into democratic offices. Existing legislation is one of the major obstacles in our path. There is no reason not to utilize what little existing power of ours we have to accelerate this process.

We will use the transition to decentralized ways of life as the vehicle to truly deliver and establish economic social and racial justice in the world. It will be a difficult, but worthy journey and step in the evolution of mankind.

Spread the word, with respect and dignity. Live and breath the philosophies of love and unity. For the first time in history, we can use technology to unite humanity while simultaneously respect our individuality.

Oh, what a beautiful time it is to be alive.
Oh, what a beautiful time.

To my family and the people around me. You know who you are.

You make life worth living.

Thank you.

"It is dangerous to be right, when the government is wrong."

Voltaire

"If you want to know who controls you, look at who you are not allowed to criticize."

Voltaire

"Those who make peaceful revolution impossible will make violent revolution inevitable."

John F. Kennedy

"The revolution is not an apple that falls when it is ripe. You have to make it fall."

Che Guevara

"When the earth is ravaged and the animals are dying, a new tribe of people shall come unto the earth from many colors, creeds, and classes, ad who, by their actions and deeds, shall make the earth green again. They shall be know as the warriors of the rainbow."

Hepsi Prophecy

"Bitcoin will remain, in my opinion, a relentless anomaly that refuses to go away - a black swan that cannot be ignored or extinguished."

Andreas M. Antonopoulos

"A tax-supported, compulsory educational system is the complete model of the totalitarian state."

Isabel Paterson

"Trusted third-parties are security holes."

Nick Szabo

"WikiLeaks has kicked the hornet's nest, and the swarm is headed towards us."

Satoshi Nakamoto

"There are almost 200 currencies of the world, but there's only one international currency. There are almost 200 currencies controlled by central banks and governments, but there is only one mathematical currency today, and that is bitcoin. We are going to build more of them. Cryptographic currencies are going to be a mainstay of our financial fu-

ture. They are going to be a part of the future of this planet because they have been invented. It's as simple as that. You cannot un-invent this technology. You cannot turn this omelette back into eggs."

Andreas M. Antonopoulos

"PayPal had these goals of creating a new currency. We failed at that, and we just created a new payment system. I think Bitcoin has succeeded on the level of a new currency, but the payment system is somewhat lacking. It's very hard to use, and that's the big challenge on the Bitcoin side."

Peter Thiel

"The reason there will be no change is because the people who stand to lose from change have all the power. And the people who stand to gain from change have none of the power."

A Summary of a section from chapter 6 of *The Prince* by *Machiavelli*

"If the machine of government is of such a nature that it requires you to be the agent of injustice to another, then, I say, break the law."

Henry David Thoreau

Notable Information

You can find the latest version of the most notable information in this book on the dedicated website:

BlockchainMaximalist.com

Thank you for your time and dedication in reading my writing. I truly appreciate your support and hope to have been able to provide some valuable insights for you.

We are all familiar of the, not only significant, but crucial impact that reviews have on the success and failure of a book in modern publishing. Which is why I must now shamelessly ask you for your time once more.

If you enjoyed this book, if you have learned something new about Blockchain and the surrounding landscape, or if the journey was engaging and entertaining for you, please leave a review on Amazon.

Thank you.

Luis

References

Introduction

Rates of inflation, U.S. Bureau of Labor Statistics, n.d. Web. 6 Feb. 2019.
<https://www.bls.gov/cpi/>.

Consumer Price Index, Coinnews Media Group LLC, n.d. Web. 6 Feb. 2019.
<https://www.usinflationcalculator.com/inflation/consumer-price-index-and-annual-percent-changes-from-1913-to-2008>.

U.S. Inflation Rate, Official Data Foundation / Alioth LLC, n.d. Web. 6 Feb. 2019.
<https://www.officialdata.org/1831-dollars-in-2018>.

Annual Inflation Rate, Eurostat, n.d. Web. 6 Feb. 2019.
<http://appsso.eurostat.ec.europa.eu/nui/show.do?dataset=prc_hicp_-manr&lang=en>.

"The 'yellow vest' movement explained." Al Jazeera and News Agencies, 4 Dec. 2018. Web. 6 Feb. 2019.
<https://www.aljazeera.com/news/2018/12/happening-france-yellow-vest-movement-explained-181204153014250.html>.

Gupta, Girish. "Venezuela 2017 annual inflation at 2,616 percent: opposition lawmakers." Reuters, 8 Jan. 2018. Web. 6 Feb. 2019.
<https://www.reuters.com/article/us-venezuela-economy-inflation/venezuela-2017-annual-inflation-at-2616-percent-opposition-lawmakers-idUSKBN1EX23B>.

Heeb, Gina. "Venezuela's inflation hits more than 40,000% as everyone dumps its currency 'like a hot potato'." *Insider Inc.* Business Insider, 30 Jun. 2018. Web. 6 Feb. 2019.
<https://www.businessinsider.com/venezuela-inflation-hits-more-than-40000-investors-dump-currency-2018-6?r=UK>.

"BlackRock Chief Larry Fink: Soaring US Deficit Will Kill Stock Rally." *Newsmax Finance.* Newsmax Media, Inc. 9 Nov. 2018. Web. 6 Feb. 2019.

<https://www.newsmax.com/finance/streettalk/blackrock-larry-fink-deficit-budget/2018/11/09/id/890133/>.

Part 1

Blockchain

Warburg, Bettina. "How the blockchain will radically transform the economy." ted.com. TED, n.d. Web. 29 Nov. 2018.
<https://www.ted.com/talks/bettina_war-burg_how_the_blockchain_will_radically_transform_the_economy/transcript?language=en>.

"What is Blockchain?." lisk.io. Lisk, n.d. Web. 26 Nov. 2018.
<https://lisk.io/academy/blockchain-basics/what-is-blockchain>.

Finley, Klint. "The wired guide to the Blockchain" *wired.com*. Condé Nast, 1 Feb. 2018. Web. 6 Feb. 2019.
<https://www.wired.com/story/guide-blockchain>.

Haber W, Stuart and Stornetta, Scott. "How to time-stamp a digital document." *Journal of Cryptology*. Springer Link, Jan. 1991. Web. 6 Feb. 2019.
<https://link.springer.com/article/10.1007/BF00196791>.

Haber W, Stuart and Stornetta, Scott. "How to time-stamp a digital document." *Journal of Cryptology*. anf.es, Jan. 1991. Web. 22 Apr. 2018.
<https://www.anf.es/pdf/Haber_Stornetta.pdf>.

Ang, Josi. "Fundamental Data Structures." *scribd.com*. Scribd Inc, 15 Jan. 2014. Web. 6 Feb. 2019.
<https://www.scribd.com/document/199819816/Fundamental-Data-Structures>.

Bayer, Dave, Haber W, Stuart and Stornetta, Scott. "Improving the Efficiency and Reliability of Digital Time-Stamping." *Sequences II*. Springer Link, 4 Jun. 2017. Web. 6 Feb. 2019.
<https://link.springer.com/chapter/10.1007/978-1-4613-9323-8_24>.

Asolo, Bisade. "Full Node and Lightweight Node" mycryptopedia.-com. Mycryptopedia, 01 Nov. 2018. Web. 29 Nov. 2018.
<https://www.mycryptopedia.com/full-node-lightweight-node/>.

The Columbia Encyclopedia, 6th ed. "Computer Program" Encyclopedia.com. The Columbia University Press, n.d. Web. 29 Nov. 2018. <https://www.encyclopedia.com/science-and-technology/computers-and-electrical-engineering/computers-and-computing/computer-program#2>.

Frankenfield, Jake. "Block Header (Cryptocurrency)" investopedia.com. Investopedia, 14 Mar. 2018. Web. 29 Nov. 2018. <https://www.investopedia.com/terms/b/block-header-cryptocurrency.asp>.

Madeira, Antonio. "What is a Block Header in Bitcoin?" cryptocompare.com. Crypto Coin Comparison Ltd, n.d. Web. 29 Nov. 2018. <https://www.cryptocompare.com/coins/guides/what-is-a-block-header-in-bitcoin>.

Pullen, John Patrick. "Macy's Black Friday Sales Hurt by Credit Card Processing Problem." fortune.com. Fortune Media IP Ltd, 25 Nov. 2017. Web. 03 Nov. 2018. <http://fortune.com/2017/11/24/macys-black-friday-sales-hurt-credit-card-processing-problem/>.

Anodot. "Macy's Black Friday Failure an Industry-Wide Problem… and Could Have Been Avoided" anodot.com. Anodot Ltd, n.d. Web. 03 Nov. 2018. <https://www.anodot.com/blog/macys-black-friday-failure-industry-wide-problemand-avoided/>.

"What is Decentralization?." lisk.io. Lisk, n.d. Web. 26 Nov. 2018. <https://lisk.io/academy/blockchain-basics/benefits-of-blockchain/what-is-decentralization>.

Frankenfield, Jake. "Difficulty (Cryptocurrencies)" investopedia.com. Investopedia, 30 Jan. 2018. Web. 03 Nov. 2018. <https://www.investopedia.com/terms/d/difficulty-cryptocurrencies.asp>.

"Difficulty" bitcoin.it. Bitcoin Wiki, 12 Apr. 2017. Web. 03 Nov. 2018. <https://en.bitcoin.it/wiki/Difficulty>.

Frankenfield, Jake. "Nonce" investopedia.com. Investopedia, 23 Oct. 2017. Web. 03 Nov. 2018. <https://www.investopedia.com/terms/n/nonce.asp>.

Sharma, Toshendra Kumar. "How does Blockchain use Public Key Cryptography?" blockchain-council.org. Blockchain Council, 27 Jan. 2018. Web. 29 Nov. 2018.
<https://www.blockchain-council.org/blockchain/how-does-blockchain-use-public-key-cryptography>.

Goldman, David. "Major banks hit with biggest cyberattacks in history" cnn.com. Cable News Network. Turner Broadcasting System, Inc, 28 Sep. 2012. Web. 09 Jul. 2018.
<https://money.cnn.com/2012/09/27/technology/bank-cyberattacks>.

"Huh, Cryptocurrencies Cryptography: How Does it All Work?" blockgeeks.com. Blockgeeks, n.d. Web. 03 Nov. 2018.
<https://blockgeeks.com/guides/cryptocurrencies-cryptography/>.

Greenspan, Alan. "Alan Greenspan on What Trump Gets Wrong and Sweden Gets Right." barrons.com. Dow Jones & Company, Inc., n.d. Web. 26 Nov. 2018.
<https://www.barrons.com/articles/alan-greenspan-interview-1539635388>.

Smart Contracts

Szabo, Nick. "Smart Contracts" fon.hum.uva.nl. 1994. Web. 19 Aug. 2017.
<http://www.fon.hum.uva.nl/rob/Courses/InformationInSpeech/CDROM/Literature/LOTwinterschool2006/szabo.best.vwh.net/smart.-contracts.html>.

Frankenfield, Jake. "Smart Contracts" investopedia.com. Investopedia, 18 Apr. 2017. Web. 19 Aug. 2017.
<https://www.investopedia.com/terms/s/smart-contracts.asp>.

Consensus Mechanisms

Dwork, Cynnthia & Naor, Moni. "Pricing via Processing or Combatting Junk Mail" wisdom.weizmann.ac.il. wisdom.weizmann.ac.il, n.d. Web. 23 Feb. 2017.

<http://www.wisdom.weizmann.ac.il/~naor/PAPERS/pvp.ps>.

"Hashcash" hashcash.org. hashcash.org, n.d. Web. 16 Dec. 2017.
<http://www.hashcash.org>.

"golem" golem.network. Golem Factory GmbH, n.d. Web. 17 Dec.
2018.
<https://golem.network>.

Vallabh, Rao. Altumea uses Blockchain to help scientists and re-
searchers buy computer processing" yourstory.com. YourStory Media
Pvt. Ltd, 15 Mar. 2018. Web. 17 Dec. 2018.
<https://yourstory.com/2018/03/altumea-uses-blockchain-help-scien-
tists-researchers-buy-computer-processing>.

Tar, Andrew. "Proof-of-Work, Explained" cointelegraph.com. Coin-
telegraph, 17 Jan. 2018. Web. 13 Sep. 2018.
<https://cointelegraph.com/explained/proof-of-work-explained>.

"Proof of Work vs Proof of Stake" blockgeeks.com. Blockgeeks, n.d.
Web. 20 Dec. 2018.
<https://blockgeeks.com/guides/proof-of-work-vs-proof-of-stake/>.

Daily Bit. "9 Types of Consensus Mechanisms That You Didn't
Know About" medium.com. The Daily Bit, 26 Apr. 2018. Web. 06
May. 2018.
<https://medium.com/the-daily-bit/9-types-of-consensus-mechanisms-
that-you-didnt-know-about-49ec365179da>.

Vasa. "ConsensusPedia: An Encyclopedia of 30+ Consensus Algorithms" hackernoon.com. Hackernoon, 02 Jul. 2018. Web. 06 May
2018.
<https://hackernoon.com/consensuspedia-an-encyclopedia-of-29-con-
sensus-algorithms-e9c4b4b7d08f>.

Deetman, Sebastiaan. "Bitcoin Could Consume as Much Electricity as
Denmark by 2020" motherboard.vice.com. Motherboard, 29 Mar.
2016. Web. 14 Jun. 2017.
<https://motherboard.vice.com/en_us/article/aek3za/bitcoin-could-
consume-as-much-electricity-as-denmark-by-2020>.

"Bitcoin Energy Consumption Index" digiconomist.net. Digiconomist,
n.d. Web. 14 Jun. 2017.
<https://digiconomist.net/bitcoin-energy-consumption>.

Concepts of Blockchain and Miscellaneous References

Coral Health. "Advanced Blockchain Concepts for Beginners" medium.com. Coral Health, 08 May. 2018. Web. 18 Nov. 2018. <https://medium.com/@mycoralhealth/advanced-blockchain-concepts-for-beginners-32887202afad>.

Morrow, Jerome. "What is a Coinbase Transaction?" blog.cex.io. CEX, 29 Oct. 2014. Web. 09 Dec. 2016. <https://blog.cex.io/bitcoin-dictionary/coinbase-transaction-12088>.

Turing, Alan. "On computable numbers, with an application to the Entscheidungsproblem." cs.virginia.edu. A.M/. Turing, 28 May. 1936. Web. 14 Nov. 2016. <https://www.cs.virginia.edu/~robins/Turing_Paper_1936.pdf>.

"Blockchain Oracles" blockchainhub.net. BlockchainHub, n.d. Web. 02 Oct. 2018. <https://blockchainhub.net/blockchain-oracles/>.

"ASIC" bitcoin.it. Bitcoin Wiki, 29 May. 2015. Web. 21 Oct. 2018. <https://en.bitcoin.it/wiki/ASIC>.

Part 2

Timeline

Lamport, Leslie, Shostak, Robert & Pease, Marshall. "The Byzantine Generals Problem" microsoft.com. Microsoft, Jul. 1982. Web. 29 Nov. 2018.
<https://www.microsoft.com/en-us/research/publication/byzantine-generals-problem/?from=http%3A%2F%2Fresearch.microsoft.com%2Fen-us%2Fum%2Fpeople%2Flamport%2Fpubs%2Fbyz.pdf>.

Kirrmann, Hubert. "Fault Tolerant Computing in Industrial Automation." web.archive.org. ABB Research Center, 2005. Web. 29 Nov. 2018.
<https://web.archive.org/web/20140326192930/http://lamspeople.epfl.ch/kirrmann/Pubs/FaultTolerance/Fault_Tolerance_Tutorial_HK.pdf>.

Chaum, David. "Blind signatures for untraceable payments" ted.com. TED, 1998. Web. 20 Dec. 2016.
<www.hit.bme.hu/~buttyan/courses/BMEVIHIM219/2009/Chaum.BlindSigForPayment.1982.PDF>.

Fiorillo, Steve. "Bitcoin History: Timeline, Origins and Founder" thestreet.com. The Street, Inc, 17 Aug. 2018. Web. 28 Aug. 2018.
<https://www.thestreet.com/investing/bitcoin/bitcoin-history-14686578>.

Frankenfield, Jake. "DigiCash" investopedia.com. Investopedia, 13 Jun. 2018. Web. 04 Sep. 2018.
<https://www.investopedia.com/terms/d/digicash.asp>.

O'leary, Martin. "The Mysterious Disappearance of Satoshi Nakamoto, Founder & Creator of Bitcoin" huffingtonpost.com. Verizon Media, 08 May. 2015. Web. 07 Apr. 2016.
<https://www.huffingtonpost.com/martin-oaleary/the-mysterious-disappeara_2_b_7217206.html?guccounter=1>.

Moskov, Philip. "What Is Bit Gold? The Brainchild of Blockchain Pioneer Nick Szabo" coincentral.com. CoinCentral, 22 May. 2018. Web. 18 Nov. 2018.
<https://coincentral.com/what-is-bit-gold-the-brainchild-of-blockchain-pioneer-nick-szabo/>.

Pearson, Jordan. "Former Bitcoin Developer Shares Early Satoshi Nakamoto Emails" motherboard.vice.com. Motherboard, 11 Aug. 2017. Web. 18 Nov. 2018.
<https://motherboard.vice.com/en_us/article/7xx9gb/former-bitcoin-developer-shares-early-satoshi-nakamoto-emails>.

"Bitcoin" coinmarketcap.com. CoinMarketCap, n.d. Web. 06 Feb. 2019.
<https://coinmarketcap.com/currencies/bitcoin/>.

"History of Ethereum" coinmama.com. Coinmama, n.d. Web. 02 Dec. 2018.
<https://www.coinmama.com/guide/history-of-ethereum>.

Norry, Andrew. "The History of the Mt. Gox Hack: Bitcoin's Biggest Heist" blockonomi.com. Blockonomi, 19 Nov. 2018. Web. 02 Dec. 2018.
<https://blockonomi.com/mt-gox-hack/>.

McLannahan, Ben. "Bitcoin exchange Mt. Gox files for bankruptcy protection" *ft.com. Financial Times*, 28 Feb. 2014. Web. 02 Dec. 2018.
<www.ft.com/intl/cms/s/0/6636e0e8-a06e-11e3-a72c-00144fe-ab7de.html#axzz2v8w0y2mI>.

Vigna, Paul. "5 Things About Mt. Gox's Crisis" *blogs.wsj.com. The Wall Street Journal*, 15 Feb.2014. Web. 02 Dec. 2018.
<https://blogs.wsj.com/five-things/2014/02/25/5-things-about-mt-goxs-crisis/>.

Abrams, Rachel, Goldstein, Matthew, and Tabuchi, Hiroko. "Erosion of Faith Was Death Knell for Mt. Gox" nytimes.com. The New York Times Company, 28 Feb. 2014. Web. 03 Dec. 2018.
<https://dealbook.nytimes.com/2014/02/28/mt-gox-files-for-bank-ruptcy/>.

Ogun, M.N. "Terrorist Use of Cyberspace and Cyber Terrorism: New Challenges and Responses" books.google.be. Google Books, 08 Oct. 2015. Web. 02 Dec. 2018.

<https://books.google.be/books?
id=oPboDAAAQBAJ&pg=PA47&dq=mt.
+gox+70&hl=en&sa=X&redir_esc=y#v=onepage&q=mt.
%20gox&f=false>.

Frunza, Marius-Christina. "Solving Modern Crime in Financial Markets: Analytics and Case Studies" books.google.be. Google Books, 09 Dec. 2015. Web. 03 Dec. 2018.
<https://books.google.com/books?
id=EokpCgAAQBAJ&pg=PA65&dq=mt.
+gox+70&hl=en&sa=X&ved=0ahUKEwiX452C5YvUAhVE7-
CYKHfiTDl4Q6AEILTAB#v=onepage&q=mt.+gox+70&f=false>.

Byford, Sam. "How the blockchain will radically transform the economy." theverge.com. Vox Media, Inc, 16 Apr. 2014. Web. 04 Dec. 2018.
<https://www.theverge.com/2014/4/16/5619636/mt-gox-asks-for-permission-to-liquidate>.

Frankenfield, Jake. "Hard Fork" investopedia.com. Investopedia, 06 Feb. 2019. Web. 06 Feb. 2019.
<https://www.investopedia.com/terms/h/hard-fork.asp>.

Farzam, Ehsani. "Blockchain in Finance: From Buzzword to Watchword in 2016" *coindesk.com*. CoinDesk, 20 Dec. 2016. Web. 12 Aug. 2018.
<https://www.coindesk.com/blockchain-finance-buzzword-watchword-2016>.

The Linux Foundation. "Linux Foundation Unites Industry Leaders to Advance Blockchain Technology" *linuxfoundation.org*. The Linux Foundation, 17 Dec. 2015. Web. 14 Oct. 2018.
<https://www.linuxfoundation.org/press-release/2015/12/linux-foundation-unites-industry-leaders-to-advance-blockchain-technology/>.

Blast Media Newsroom. "2016: A Year of Milestones for Bitcoin" blastmagazine.com. Blast Media Newsroom, 04 Dec. 2016. Web. 15 Oct. 2018.
<https://blastmagazine.com/2016/12/04/2016-year-milestones-bitcoin/
>.

Tozzi, Christopher. "2017 Milestones in the World of Bitcoin and Blockchain" channelfutures.com. Channel Futures, 04 Dec. 2017. Web. 29 Nov. 2018.

<https://www.channelfutures.com/channel-futures/2017-milestones-world-bitcoin-and-blockchain>.

Alexandre, Ana. "New Study Says 80 Percent of ICOs Conducted in 2017 Were Scams" cointelegraph.com. Coin Telegraph, 13 Jul. 2018. Web. 09 Sep. 2018. <https://cointelegraph.com/news/new-study-says-80-percent-of-icos-conducted-in-2017-were-scams>.

XBT Network. "Bitcoin (BTC): Best & Worst Things That Happened To Date In 2018" *xbt.net.* XBT.net, 29 May. 2018. Web. 10 Sep. 2018. <https://stocksgazette.com/2018/05/29/bitcoin-btc-best-worst-things-that-happened-in-2018/>.

Blockchain Technology Benefits And Challenges and Miscellaneous References

"Blockchain Technology: Benefits and Challenges" proshareng.com. Proshare, 02 Apr. 2018. Web. 26 July. 2018. <https://www.proshareng.com/news/%20BlockChain%20&%20Cryptos/Blockchain-Technology--Benefits-and-Challenges/39224>.

"The great chain of being sure about things" economist.com. The Economist Newspaper Ltd, 31 Oct. 2015. Web. 26 Jul. 2018. <https://www.economist.com/briefing/2015/10/31/the-great-chain-of-being-sure-about-things>.

Popper, Nathaniel. "A Venture Fund With Plenty of Virtual Capital, but No Capitalist." nytimes.com. The New York Times Company, 21 May. 2016. Web. 27 Jul. 2018. <https://www.nytimes.com/2016/05/22/business/dealbook/crypto-ether-bitcoin-currency.html>.

Iansiti, Marco & Lakhani, Karim R. "The Truth About Blockchain" hbr.org. Harvard Business School Publishing, Jan 2017. Web. 28 Jul. 2018. <https://hbr.org/2017/01/the-truth-about-blockchain>.

Part 3

Decentralized Economics

Fagella, Dan. "Self-driving car timeline for 11 top automakers." *venturebeat.com*. VentureBeat, 4 Jun. 2017. Web. 6 Feb. 2019. <https://venturebeat.com/2017/06/04/self-driving-car-timeline-for-11-top-automakers>.

Austin Bohlig, Gene Munster,. "Auto Outlook 2040: The Rise of Fully Autonomous Vehicles." *loupventures.com*. Loup Ventures, 6 Nov. 2017. Web. 6 Feb. 2019. <https://loupventures.com/auto-outlook-2040-the-rise-of-fully-autonomous-vehicles>.

Blockchain Education System

Clark, Donald. "10 ways Blockchain could be used in education." *oeb.global*. OEB Newsportal, 12 Nov. 2016. Web. 6 Feb. 2019. <https://oeb.global/oeb-insights/10-ways-blockchain-could-be-used-in-education>.

Tan, Wen Chuan. "Blockchain could revolutionize education next. Here's how." *quantrivakhoinghiep.org*. Tech in Asia, 23 Jul. 2018. Web. 6 Feb. 2019. <https://www.techinasia.com/blockchain-revolution-education>.

Phukan, Pranjal Kumar. "Prospects of Block Chain Technology in Education." *nelive.in*. Nelive, 19 Jul. 2018. Web. 7 Feb. 2019. <https://www.nelive.in/assam/education/prospects-block-chain-technology-education>.

Blockchain Governance

Staff Reports. "How Many Democratic Nations Are There?" borgenmagazine.com. The Borgen Project, 29 Sep. 2013. Web. 08 Oct. 2018.

<https://www.borgenmagazine.com/many-democratic-nations/>.

Tozzi, Christopher. "Blockchain Voting Comes to America: West Virginia's Voatz Experiment" nasdaq.com. Nasdaq.com, 04 Oct. 2018. Web. 12 Dec. 2018.
<https://www.nasdaq.com/article/blockchain-voting-comes-to-america-west-virginias-voatz-experiment-cm1032115>.

Coleman, Lauren deLisa. "Inside The Hot Discussion On Blockchain And The Chaos Of Mid-Term Election Recounts" forbes.com. Forbes Media LLC, 11 Nov. 2018. Web. 12 Nov. 2018.
<https://www.forbes.com/sites/laurencoleman/2018/11/11/inside-the-hot-discussion-on-blockchain-and-the-chaos-of-mid-term-election-recounts/#3d8107cb31fa>.

Meyer, David. "Blockchain Voting Notches Another Success—This Time in Switzerland" http://fortune.com. Fortune Media IP Ltd, 03 Jul. 2018. Web. 14 Oct. 2018.
<http://fortune.com/2018/07/03/blockchain-voting-trial-zug/>.

Beedham, Mathhew. "Japan is experimenting with a blockchain-powered voting system" thenextweb.com. TNW Remarkable Progress, 03 Sep. 2018. Web. 14 Oct. 2018.
<https://thenextweb.com/hardfork/2018/09/03/japan-city-blockchain-voting/>.

Coggine, Anthony. "State of Illinois Sponsors Month-Long Blockchain Hackathon" cointelegraph.com. Coin Telegraph, 22 Jun. 2017. Web. 03 Sep. 2018.
<https://cointelegraph.com/news/state-of-illinois-sponsors-month-long-blockchain-hackathon>.

Alois, JD. "Crypto Rockies: Wyoming Continues Legislative March to Create a Blockchain Friendly Market with Digital Asset Property Law" *crowdfundinsider.com*. Crowded Media Group, 15 Feb. 2019. Web. 15 Feb. 2019.
<https://cointelegraph.com/news/finally-state-of-delaware-passes-important-bill-for-blockchain-technology>.

Coggine, Anthony. "Finally, State of Delaware Passes Important Bill for Blockchain Technology" *cointelegraph.com*. Coin Telegraph, 03 Jul. 2017. Web. 04 Sep. 2018.

<https://www.crowdfundinsider.com/2019/02/144553-crypto-rockies-wyoming-continues-legislative-march-to-create-a-blockchain-friendly-market-with-digital-asset-property-law/>.

Breuer, Hubertus. "New York neighbours power up blockchain-based Brooklyn Microgrid" *siliconrepublic.com*. Silicone Republic, 27 Sep. 2017. Web. 04 Sep. 2018. <https://www.siliconrepublic.com/machines/brooklyn-microgrid-blockchain-energy-networks>.

Holder, Sarah. "Is This Experiment in Digital Democracy Too Crazy to Work?" citylab.com. The Atlantic Monthly Group, 11 Sep. 2018. Web. 14 Oct. 2018. <https://www.citylab.com/life/2018/09/is-this-west-virginia-experiment-in-digital-democracy-crazy/569542/>.

"Tsukuba first in Japan to deploy online voting system" japantimes.co.jp. The Japan Times Ltd, 02 Sep. 2018. Web. 15 Oct. 2018. <https://www.japantimes.co.jp/news/2018/09/02/national/politics-diplomacy/new-online-voting-system-introduced-city-tsukuba/#.W4y65pMzZbV>.

Jenkinson, Gareth. "Blockchain and Energy - Two Peas In a Pod" cointelegraph.com. Coin Telegraph, 07 Feb. 2018. Web. 29 May. 2018. <https://cointelegraph.com/news/blockchain-and-energy-two-peas-in-a-pod>.

Huillet, Marie. "IBM Signs $740 Million Deal With Australian Gov't to Use Blockchain for Data Security." cointelegraph.com. Coin Telegraph, 05 Jul. 2018. Web. 07 Oct. 2018. <https://cointelegraph.com/news/ibm-signs-740-million-deal-with-australian-gov-t-to-use-blockchain-for-data-security>.

"Smart Dubai." smartdubai.ae. Smart Dubai, n.d. Web. 08 Oct. 2018. <https://smartdubai.ae/initiatives/blockchain>.

D'Cunha, Suparna Dutt. "Dubai Sets Its Sights On Becoming The World's First Blockchain-Powered Government" forbes.com. Forbes, 18 Dec. 2017. Web. 08 Oct. 2018. <https://www.forbes.com/sites/suparnadutt/2017/12/18/dubai-sets-sights-on-becoming-the-worlds-first-blockchain-powered-government/#62cd2b19454b>.

Kramer, Melanie. "Dubai is building a Blockchain-powered government" bitcoinist.com. Bitcoinist.com, 24 Sep. 2018. Web. 09 Oct. 2018.
<https://bitcoinist.com/dubai-is-building-a-blockchain-powered-government/>.

Young, Joseph. "Suddenly, Dubai Aims to Become First Blockchain-Powered City by 2020" cointelegraph.com. Coin Telegraph, 21 Feb. 2017. Web. 09 Oct. 2018.
<https://cointelegraph.com/news/suddenly-dubai-aims-to-become-first-blockchain-powered-city-by-2020>.

Magas, Julia. "Smart Cities and Blockchain: Four Countries Where AI and DLT Exist Hand-in-Hand" cointelegraph.com. Coin Telegraph, 17 Jun. 2018. Web. 12 Oct. 2018.
<https://cointelegraph.com/news/smart-cities-and-blockchain-four-countries-where-ai-and-dlt-exist-hand-in-hand>.

Police and Surveillance

Tsolakidou, Stella. "The Police in Ancient Greece" greekreporter.com. GreekReporter.com, 30 May. 2013. Web. 14 Mar. 2017.
<https://greece.greekreporter.com/2013/05/30/the-police-in-ancient-greece/>.

Whitehouse, David. "Origins of the police" worxintheory.wordpress.com. WorkinTheory, 07 Dec. 2014. Web. 14 Mar. 2017.
<https://worxintheory.wordpress.com/2014/12/07/origins-of-the-police/>.

Sanburn, Josh. "The One Battle Michael Brown's Family Will Win" time.com. Time USA, LLC, 26 Nov. 2014. Web. 15 Mar. 2017
<http://time.com/3606376/police-cameras-ferguson-evidence/>.

"Law enforcement & police body cameras" revealmedia.com. Reveal Media, n.d. Web. 15 Mar. 2017.
<https://www.revealmedia.com/int/police-body-worn-cameras>.

Honig, Dan & Johnson, Jayme. "Body Cameras Work – Just Not in the Way You Think" policefoundation.org. Police Foundation, n.d. Web. 15 Aug. 2018.

<https://www.policefoundation.org/body-cameras-work-just-not-in-the-way-you-think/>.

Deyner, Simon. "China bets on facial recognition in big drive for total surveillance" washingtonpost.com. The Washington post, 07 Jan, 2018. Web. 15 Aug. 2018.
<https://www.washingtonpost.com/news/world/wp/2018/01/07/feature/in-china-facial-recognition-is-sharp-end-of-a-drive-for-total-surveillance/>.

Mozur, Paul. "Inside China's Dystopian Dreams: A.I., Shame and Lots of Cameras" nytimes.com. The New York Times Company, 08 Jul, 2018. Web. 16 Aug. 2018.
<https://www.nytimes.com/2018/07/08/business/china-surveillance-technology.html>.

Political Philosophy

A. "Do we need or want any form of government?" *theanarchistlibrary.org*. The Anarchist Library, A pamphlet, 1983. Web. 04 Sep. 2017.
<https://theanarchistlibrary.org/library/a-do-we-need-or-want-any-form-of-government>.

Bederka, Travis James. "Do We Need Government?" *theodysseyonline.com*. The Odyssey, 12 Jan 2017. Web. 04 Sep. 2017.
<https://www.theodysseyonline.com/do-we-need-government>.

McCarthy, Niall. "1.7 Billion Adults Worldwide Do Not Have Access To A Bank Account" *forbes.com*. Forbes Media LLC, 08 Jun 2018. Web. 04 Sep. 2017.
<https://www.forbes.com/sites/mypos/2019/01/24/a-smarter-way-to-do-retail/#96499c211286>.

Intense

Storrow, Bejamin. "Global CO2 Emissions Rise after Paris Climate Agreement Signed" *scientificamerican.com*. Scientific American, a Division of Springer Nature America Inc, 24 Mar. 2018. Web. 6 Feb. 2019.
<https://www.scientificamerican.com/article/global-co2-emissions-rise-after-paris-climate-agreement-signed/>.

"It is not because things are difficult that we do not dare;

it is because we do not dare that things are difficult."

Seneca

Made in the USA
Coppell, TX
21 December 2020